■

Michael Gerber's *E-Myth* is one of only four books I recommend as required reading. **For those looking to start and build a business of their own, this is the man who has coached more successful entrepreneurs than the next ten gurus combined.**

—Timothy Ferriss, #1 *New York Times* bestselling author of *The 4-Hour Work Week*

**Michael Gerber's *Awakening the Entrepreneur Within* is thought provoking and revolutionary.** It will make you laugh and cry, become angry, uncomfortable, challenged, energized, elated, and inspired to bring new meaning and purpose to your life and your business. **If you want to imagine and pursue a business and a life that transforms the world, then this book should be your bible.** You'll read his empowering words time and time again. **There is no other business book of its kind** and no other dreamer like Michael Gerber. I am confident it will change your life.

—Susan Wilson Solovic, CEO, SBTV.com, and author of
*The Girls' Guide to Building a Million-Dollar Business*

Everyone needs a mentor, someone who tells it like it is, holds you accountable, and shows you your good, bad, and ugly. For millions of small business owners Michael Gerber is that person. **Let Michael be your mentor and you are in for a kick in the pants, the ride of a lifetime.**

—John Jantsch, author of *Duct Tape Marketing*

Since the groundbreaking *E-Myth* series, the business world has been waiting for the next paradigm-shattering offering from business legend Michael Gerber. Now finally it is here, and it is called *Awakening the Entrepreneur Within*. Based on his remarkable Dreaming Room programs, this book will show you exactly how to awaken and reenergize the entrepreneur within you. **When Michael Gerber talks every business person should listen. Get this book!**

—Mitch Meyerson, author of *Mastering Online Marketing*
and founder of Guerrilla Marketing Coaching

Only read this book if you want to do big things in the world. By the time you finish the first chapter you won't have a choice anymore. **Michael Gerber and this book hold the keys to making your dreams come true.**

—Michael Port, author of *Book Yourself Solid* and *Beyond Booked Solid*

**Michael Gerber has transformed my life through the powerful message of *Awakening the Entrepreneur Within*.** By following Michael's advice, I have taken my entrepreneurial goals to a much higher level. Michael is the world's leading voice in entrepreneurship and **this book is a must read for anyone serious about taking control of their life.**

—Kevin Pringles, president, Chill Factor Clothing Co.

Michael Gerber's *E-Myth* books redefined what true business and entrepreneurship is all about, freeing business owners everywhere from the prison of their own making. Now, in his new book, he has taken the next bold step of showing people how to tap into their true sense of purpose and live it through enlightened entrepreneurship, resulting in a much better world for all. ***Awakening the Entrepreneur Within* could easily become one of the most important business and sociological books of our time.**

—Michael J. Russer, author of *The Obsolete Employee:
How Businesses Succeed Without Employees—And Love It!*

My shelves are crammed with thirty years of accumulated business books—all of them telling me how to do this-or-that, more, better, or differently. I'm going to put most of them in a yard sale so that *Awakening the Entrepreneur Within* can have its rightful place of prominence. **If you want to create an extraordinary business or are wondering where to start,** *Awakening the Entrepreneur Within* **is the road map you've been seeking, but never knew you were missing—until now.**

—Steve Gottry, author of *Common Sense Business* and co-author
(with Ken Blanchard) of *The On-Time, On-Target Manager*

**Michael Gerber is a master instructor and a leader's leader.** As a combat F15 fighter pilot, I had to navigate complex missions with life-and-death consequences, but until I read *The E-Myth* and met Michael Gerber, my transition to the world of small business was a nightmare with no real flight plan. **The hands-on, practical magic of Michael's turnkey systems magnified by the raw power of his keen insight and wisdom have changed my life forever.** Michael's Dreaming Room led me to create my business with a clear vision, compelling purpose and meaningful mission. Michael, thank you for writing this book and challenging us to get in the game, to passionately pursue our dream, and to never, ever give up.

—Steve Olds, CEO, Stratworx.com

Michael Gerber's strategies in *The E-Myth* were instrumental in building my company from two employees to a global organization; I can't wait to see how applying the strategies from *Awakening the Entrepreneur Within* will affect its growth!

—Dr. Ivan Misner, founder and chairman of BNI, and author of *Masters of Sales*

Michael Gerber's gift to isolate the issues and present simple, direct, business changing solutions shines bright with *Awakening the Entre-*

*preneur Within.* **If you're interested in developing an entrepreneurial vision and plan that inspires others to action, buy this book, read it, and apply the processes Gerber brilliantly defines.**

—Tim Templeton, author of *The Referral of a Lifetime*

**Michael Gerber truly, truly understands what it takes to be a successful practicing entrepreneur and business owner.** He has demonstrated to me over six years of working with him that for those who stay the course and learn much more than just "how to work on their business and not in it" then they will reap rich rewards. I finally franchised my business and the key to unlocking this kind of potential in any business idea is in the teachings of Michael's work.

—Chris Owen, marketing director, Royal Armouries (International) plc

My wife, Colleen, and I spent twenty-five years flying in the United States Air Force and with commercial airlines. When we changed our career focus and decided to open our own business, we read dozens of books and attended countless seminars. Nothing came close to the quality and precision of the environment that we had lived in for all those years—until we read Michael Gerber's books. His insightful writings finally gave us the flight plan that we had been missing. **We carry copies of his books in our car and share them with other entrepreneurs, because we know that their lives and businesses can be changed in a profound way by the wisdom of Michael Gerber.**

—Bill and Colleen Hensley, founders of Hensley Properties, Inc.,

authors of the upcoming book, *The Pilot-Learning Leadership*

Michael's work has been an inspiration to us. His books have helped us get free from the out-of-control life that we once had. His nononsense approach kept us focused on our ultimate aim rather than day-to-day stresses. He has helped take our business to levels we couldn't have imagined possible. In the Dreaming Room made us totally reevaluate how we thought about our business and our life. **We have now redesigned our life so we can manifest the dreams we unearthed in Michael's Dreaming Room.**

—Jo and Steve Davison, founders of The Spinal Health Clinic Chiropractic Group and www.your-dream-life.com

I have been a Michael Gerber fan since the E-Myth transformed my business and my life. Recently, I attended the Dreaming Room. I was feeling stuck and limited by my own fears. **Through intentional dreaming, Michael gave me a new horizon as an entrepreneur.** I experienced the power of vision. This shift in thinking has sparked energy and given me the courage to take risks. I have become a leader with focus and I can see all the possibilities.

—Elena Rivera MacGregor, Rivera Design Group Ltd., riveradesign.com

**If you're looking for inspiration, information, or simply real world methods to take your entrepreneurial business to the next level, then your search is over!** Michael Gerber will help you realize your dreams, steer you past the obstacles, and guide you to achievement. Why would I say this? Simple! **That's what he's done (and still does) for me.**

—Peter Thomson, Peter Thomson International plc

Michael Gerber made us realize that conscious dreaming was possible and that we could do it deliberately. We're constantly aware of opportunities we could be dreaming about and how to improve services and products for people that would make their life better and bring profit to us. Thank you, Michael!

—Pam and Phil Reed, owners, The Reed Team, Willis Allen Real Estate, La Jolla, CA

Rarely—maybe once in a lifetime—is there a message that transforms us, that inspires us to create the vision that describes the grandest version of ourselves, and then act upon it. Several years ago, we heard such a message, Michael Gerber's message. Since then, our journey with Michael has truly awakened the entrepreneur within us! **We can't wait to take our lives and the lives of our clients to the next level through this book!**

—Robert and Susan Clements, principals, E-Myth Iowa

**Because of Michael Gerber, I transformed my twenty-four-hour-a-day, seven-day-a-week job (also called a small business) into a multimillion turnkey business.** This in turn set the foundation for my worldwide training firm. I am living my dream because of Michael Gerber.

—Howard Partridge, Phenomenal Products, Inc.

**Michael Gerber is an outrageous revolutionary who is changing the way the world does business.** He dares you to commit to your grandest dreams and then shows you how to make the impossible a reality. If you let him, this man will change your life.

—Fiona Fallon, founder of Divine and the Bottom Line

Michael Gerber is a genius. **Every successful business person I meet has read Michael Gerber, refers to Michael Gerber and lives by his words.** You just can't get enough of Michael Gerber. He has the innate (and rare) ability to tap into one's soul, look deeply, and tell you what you need to hear. And then, he inspires you, equips you with the tools to get it done.

—Pauline O'Malley, CEO, TheRevenueBuilder

**When asked "Who was the most influential person in your life?" I am one of thousands who don't hesitate to say "Michael E. Gerber."** Michael helped transform me from someone dreaming of retirement to someone dreaming of working until age one hundred. This awakening is the predictable outcome of anyone reading Michael's new book.

—Thomas O. Bardeen

**Michael Gerber is an incredible business philosopher,** guru, perhaps even a seer. He has an amazing intuition which allows him to see in an instant what everybody else is missing: he sees opportunity everywhere. While in the Dreaming Room, Michael gave me the gift of seeing through the eyes of an awakened entrepreneur, and instantly my business changed from a regional success to serving clients on four continents.

—Keith G. Schiehl, president, Rent-a-Geek Computer Services

**Michael Gerber is among the very few who truly understand entrepreneurship and small business.** While others talk about these topics in the form of theories, methodologies, processes, and so on, Michael goes to the heart of the issues. Whenever Michael writes about entrepreneurship, soak it in as it is not only good for your business, but great for your soul. His words will help you to keep your passion and balance while sailing through the uncertain sea of entrepreneuring.

—Raymond Yeh, co-author, *The Art of Business*

*Awakening the Entrepreneur Within* **is a must-read for every entrepreneur.** Michael Gerber's insight, wisdom, caring, and straightforward approach helped me reinvent myself and my business while doubling my revenues in less than one year. Crack open this book and let him do the same for you, too.

—Christine Kloser, author, *The Freedom Formula* and *Conscious Entrepreneurs*

**Michael Gerber forced me to think big, think real, and gave me the support network to make it happen.** A new wave of entrepreneurs is rising, much in thanks to his amazing efforts and very practical approach to doing business.

—Christian Kessner, Higher Ground Retreats and Events

**Michael's understanding of entrepreneurship and small business management has been a difference maker for countless businesses,**

**including Infusion Software.** His insights into the entrepreneurial process of building a business are a must read for every small business owner. The vision, clarity, and leadership that came out of our Dreaming Room experience were just what our company needed to recognize our potential and motivate the whole company to achieve it.

—Clate Mask, president and CEO, Infusion Software

Michael Gerber is a truly remarkable man. His steady openness of mind and ability to get to the deeper level continues to be an inspiration and encouragement to me. He seems to always ask that one question that forces the new perspective to break open and he approaches the new coming method in a fearless way.

—Rabbi Levi Cunin, Chabad of Malibu

The Dreaming Room experience was literally life changing for us. Within months, we were able to start our Foundation and make several television appearances owing to his teachings. He has an incredible charisma which is priceless, but above all **Michael Gerber** *awakens* **passion from within enabling you to take action with dramatic results . . . starting today!**

—Shona and Shaun Carcary, Trinity Property Investments Inc.—
Home Vestors franchisees

I thought *E-Myth* was an awkward name! What could this book do for me? But when I finally got to reading it . . . it was what I was looking for all along. Then, to top it off, I took a twenty-seven-hour trip to San Diego just to attend the Dreaming Room, where Michael touched my heart, my mind, and my soul.

—Helmi Natto, president, Eye 2 Eye Optics, Saudi Arabia

I attended *In the Dreaming Room* and was challenged by Michael Gerber to "Go out and do what's impossible." So I did: I became an author and international speaker and used Michael's principles to create a world-class company that will change and save lives all over the world.

—Dr. Don Kennedy, MBA, author, *5AM & Already Behind*,

www.bahabits.com

This book should carry a health warning. If you have only experienced success and fortune in your business, it might not appeal to you; unless you have stared in the eyes of the abyss—laughed and roared because you were too scared to do anything else—some of this will not relate to you. Sometimes you concluding what is the truth—is just you not having to look hard enough. And when you have, **read Michael Gerber's excellent work and you can start becoming a true human being who in a commercial way wants to change the world, with heart.**

—Jan Eskildsen, managing director, Paper4u Ltd

Entrepreneurs are a strange breed. We work crazy hours, take risks that others would never consider and work for nothing till our business grows. When we succeed people say that we are "lucky" or "in the right place at the right time." **The truth is we have a great coach and an incredible mentor who has awakened our entrepreneur within: Michael Gerber, the entrepreneur's secret weapon.**

—Patrick W. J. Davies, owner of Town & Country Tree Service,

and awakened entrepreneur

**Michael Gerber leads you on a journey to discover your greatest desire and helps you gather the confidence to pursue those dreams.** All you need is the courage to stay the course.

—Lisa Salt, The Salt Team, Re/Max Vernon

**As an entrepreneur and a person, Michael Gerber has given me a life lesson that I will never forget.** His words invigorate, empower, and enchant me every time I hear them. I cherish the time I get to spend with him. His E-Myth and Dreaming Room are the beacons of my journey to fulfilling my dreams.

—Merlin U. Ward

**The experience of Michael Gerber's** *Awakening the Entrepreneur Within* **is what realigned and saved my life.** Michael's extraordinary wisdom about human nature and his vast knowledge of small business became my pivots for defining, designing, and creating the future, for building the desired life and not just a business that works better. In less than two years I was transformed from a person who avoided business at all costs (an ultimate technician) to a person with two present businesses, four more in the making and many more opportunities to consider.

—Dr. Kayvon Khalilzadeh, evolutionist, Chief Creator, Interface, Parascope Technology, Inc.

**In** *Awakening the Entrepreneur Within*, **Michael Gerber answers the question, "What's beyond the E-Myth?" Once again his insights are so obvious they stare us in the face every day, and it's pure genius!**

—Mike Doughty, managing director, The Knowledge Gym

**From the moment that Michael Gerber crossed my path . . . everything changed for me.** Setting my foot into the Dreaming Room was the first step on my path to success.

—Yvonne Hoogeveen, C.I.T., president, Global Infrared Diagnostics, Ltd.

Michael Gerber is unlike anyone you know, and his biting honesty and tremendous passion enables him to transform your life. *Awakening the Entrepreneur Within* **is a triumph, the absolute pinnacle of entrepreneurial empowerment!** It should have been impossible for a book to accomplish what *Awakening* did for me, but Michael Gerber found a way.

—Peter Leeds, Penny Stock Professional, PeterLeeds.com

Michael Gerber's *E-Myth* changed and radically challenged everything I thought I knew about business. In further pursuing his life's mission of entrepreneurial innovation, Michael has now extended the lessons conveyed in the *E-Myth* to address a new and poignant observation about entrepreneurs and the companies that they envision . . . a process known as Intentional Dreaming. In response to the desperate burn-out, confusion, and pain he has witnessed in the thousands of business leaders he's worked with, **Michael has in a singular stroke provided us with a process that we can engage with to define and refine our dream.**

—Elizabeth Allen, principal, Marketsmartz, Inc.

**Michael Gerber takes us along a journey to the dreams which create businesses that change the world!** Read if, and only if, you wish to create a dream and a meaningful business that serves you with the intention of changing the world.

—Jim Aamodt, president and CEO, JDA Enterprises

Throughout my professional career, before reading *Awakening the Entrepreneur Within*, I had never picked up a book that touched me in such a personal way and managed to equally inspire and empower me with ideas and strategies that I could take into my own businesses. **This is a must read and one of the best business books I have ever read.**

—Ingrid V. Vanderveldt, Vanderveldt & Co., CEO, The Club E Network,

host CNBC's *American Made*

**Michael has never ceased to amaze me! He is by far the most brilliant speaker, author, and business consultant I've ever met.** His many years of business experience, combined with a strong intuitive nature, and truly loving intentions, combine to make a very thought-provoking, and emotionally moving message that is sure to revolutionize our world.

—Lloyd Minthorne, owner, Synoptic Sounds

Michael has an amazing way of awakening not only the entrepreneur within but the spirit so many of us lose along the way. In *The E-Myth*, Michael took a systematic approach to business success. Now he reminds us that a system without passion and soul is not worth creating. It is combining the two approaches that allows anyone to live their dreams.

—Shay Pausa, founder, ChiKiiTV and www.chikii.com

By enabling you to look closely at your business and focus on the things that matter, Gerber reminds us that life is about pursuing meaning in everything you do, personally and professionally. **You will be forever changed.**

—Kathy Sacks, founder, Sacks Public Relations

**I can easily say that Michael Gerber has been the single most influential force in the life of my business.** This is the world's opportunity to get inside the head of one the most thought-provoking business leaders the world has ever known. **Read this book. It will change your business. It will change your life.**

—Corey Blake, chairman of the dream, Writers of the Round Table, Inc.

Michael Gerber and his In the Dreaming Room concept has honestly revolutionized the way I see entrepreneurial business. **Michael will leave you energized, inspired, and prepared to make waves.**

—David Cohen, chief executive maestro, Writers of the Round Table, Inc.

I went to the Dreaming Room to have Michael Gerber fix my business. He talked about Dreaming. What was this Dreaming? I was too busy working! Too busy being miserable, angry, frustrated, behind in what I was trying to accomplish. And losing everything I was working for. Then **Michael Gerber woke up the dreamer in me and remade my life and my business.**

—Pat Doorn, president, Mountain View Electric Ltd.

Michael Gerber is brilliant. Whether you are just starting a business, or have been in business for years, **Michael has the ability to free up your thinking, explode your self-imposed limitations, then provide a razor-sharp reality check and true clarity.** Michael is a true blessing to the entrepreneur in all of us!

—Betsi Bixby, president, Meridian Associates, Inc.

I take Michael's vision of the purpose-driven entrepreneur very seriously. The journey is just beginning and I am now focused on becoming a strong entrepreneur and creating extraordinary companies. **Michael Gerber helps people understand who they are currently, and who they can become if only they dream. The results are amazing.**

—Bob Walker, co-founder, Postalcenter.com

Michael Gerber is masterful in challenging the human senses as he works to awaken the entrepreneurs within us. **Be prepared to be torn from your comfort zone and open to the flow of new ideas.**

—Larry Cooper, founder, Meetings and Events, LLC

*The E-Myth Revisited* literally changed my life by reinventing my business. Now, attending In the Dreaming Room has taken me full circle by clarifiying and articulating my Dream, Vision, Purpose, and Mission for my business with amazing precision and energy!

—Ed Herbert, chairman and CEO, Real Estate Only

Michael Gerber is, beyond any doubt, one of the most influential people I have ever met. Attending one of his Dreaming Rooms literally put my life on a brand new course. I am in the process of accomplishing a lifelong dream of starting my own business due to that event. It's a battle at times, but everything worthwhile in this life is a battle. Very soon my business will be online, and that will only be the first chapter in the business I intend to create.

—Charlie Lorance, DreamCarDriver.com

Michael Gerber's approach to life is not just measurable and sustainable, it is dignified. Like most businesses, most charities, even with the best of intents, will continue to fail, unless they have such a system as this. Where else can this be applied in your life? Come to the Dreaming Room to find out.

—Lawrence Keenan, Rose Charities Micro-Lending Project,

Vancouver, British Columbia

Michael Gerber can captivate a room full of entrepreneurs and take them to a place where they can focus on the essentials that are the underpinning of every successful business. He gently leads them from where they are to where they need to be in order to change the world.

—Francine Hardaway, CEO, Stealthmode Partners and founder

of the Arizona Entrepreneurship Conferences

# Awakening

the

## Entrepreneur Within

ALSO BY MICHAEL E. GERBER

*The E-Myth Revisited*
*E-Myth Mastery*
*The E-Myth Manager*
*The E-Myth Contractor*
*The E-Myth Physician*

# Awakening
## the
# Entrepreneur Within

*How Ordinary People*
*Can Create*
*Extraordinary Companies*

# MICHAEL E. GERBER

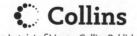

**Collins**
*An Imprint of HarperCollinsPublishers*

HarperCollins books may be purchased for educational, business, or sales promotional use. For information, please write: Special Markets Department, HarperCollins Publishers, 10 East 53rd Street, New York, NY 10022.

FIRST EDITION

*Designed by Jaime Putorti*

Library of Congress Cataloging-in-Publication Data

Gerber, Michael E.
   Awakening the entrepreneur within : how ordinary people can create extraordinary companies / Michael E. Gerber.—1st ed.
      p.   cm.
   ISBN 978-0-06-156814-5
   1. Entrepreneurship.   2. Businesspeople.   3. Creative ability in business.
4. Leadership.   5. Success in business.   I. Title.
HB615.G467   2008
658.1'1—dc22                                                    2007048755

08   09   10   11   12   DIX/RRD   10  9  8  7  6  5  4  3  2  1

*To Luz Delia . . . my wife, my lover, my partner, my friend . . .*
*Your heart is the fuel that feeds my mind.*

# ACKNOWLEDGMENTS

To my mother, Helen, whose heart, beauty and grace are unquestionably divinely inspired.

To Steve Hanselman, my agent and friend, for listening to me when you didn't want to.

To Steve Gottry, my editor and ally, for doing even more than you promised you would.

To Ethan Friedman, my "guy at Harper," for believing in this book as much as I did.

And to Steve Ross for recognizing that Harper and I were destined to work together.

To Mark Ehrlich, my friend and chief negotiator, whose determination, love, and zealous intent it is to bring The Dreaming Room to everyone in the world.

To you dear Intentional Dreamers (you know who you are!), for staying the course when you least understood why.

To you E-Myth fanatics, wherever you are, for believing in me even when I had stopped believing in me, and for passing the word.

To you, all my faithful readers, who have stayed with me through all the ups and downs, the challenges and the doubts, the dire threats and the exuberances . . . how could any of us have succeeded at all without God, the Sublime, and His Universal Laws?

And, to my children: Axel, Kim, Hillary, Sam, and Alyx; I'm sure there will be a time either in this life or the next when all of our disagreements will disappear to be seen for what they are: shifting shadows on the sublime light of God.

And to my newest children, Amethyst, Lynnez, and LuVenus, isn't this journey the strangest one of all?

And, finally, to my dear sparkling warriors of Chabad, whose spirit is never ending, whose force is to be reckoned with, whose utter joy is a constant amazement, and whose Dream of Moshiach is, as always, here and now, my Love, my commitment, my ever arising awe at your everlasting courage . . . L'Chaim.

# CONTENTS

## PART THREE: THE THINKER AND THE VISION

■

## PART FOUR: THE STORYTELLER AND THE PURPOSE

■

## PART FIVE: THE LEADER AND THE MISSION

■

# FOREWORD

In 1976, my wife Margie and I came to California on a sabbatical leave. I had just been promoted to full professor with tenure at the University of Massachusetts and Margie had just completed her Ph.D. there. Our intention was to stay in California for one year. That was more than thirty years ago. What happened? We caught the entrepreneurial bug. We decided to start our own leadership training and development company to pursue our dream of working with people we loved, making a difference in the world, and having fun. At that time we couldn't even spell the word "entrepreneur," and now we are ones! With offices in Escondido, California, Toronto, and London, plus partnerships in thirty nations, we have three hundred people working with us. By all standards we have been successful but, boy, has it been a bumpy ride.

It wasn't until the 1980s that we began getting on top of our finances. Our accountant told us we had probably been out of business several times but didn't know it. Three different times we brought in top managers from the outside, only to be disappointed and forced to take over leadership again. It would have been so helpful if Michael Gerber had been an ongoing consultant to us. It would have been a much smoother ride.

Michael Gerber has been widely regarded as "the world's number-one small business guru." That could appear to be an exaggeration, but I'm here to tell you it's not! Michael's bestselling *E-Myth* books have helped countless readers transform dreams into workable ideas, ideas into empires, and even failing companies into resounding successes. Now, in *Awakening the Entrepreneur Within*, he grabs your heart, mind, and entire psyche all at once to show you how you can enter the Dreaming Room and create the previously unimaginable. I had so many "Aha!" moments while reading this book that I simply could not set it aside until I had absorbed every word. It could—no, it *will*—be your personal awakening; your life changer. If you are already an entrepreneur, it will help you be better. If you are thinking of pursuing an entrepreneurial dream, it will help you not fail. Enjoy the ride with Michael Gerber as your conductor.

—Ken Blanchard,
co-author of *The One Minute Manager*®
and *The One Minute Entrepreneur*™

# PREFACE

If man knew that he never ceases creating even for an
instant, he would realize through the Presence of God
within himself, he could purify his miscreations
and thus be free from his own limitations.

—Godfre Ray King, *Unveiled Mysteries*

Books are born just like a business is born. In the imagination.
Books are sired by the Imagination, mothered by the Heart, then nurtured by the Intellect. In the end, the book is born, not created.

The book that follows is just such a birth.

It has come into being to live its life among you. But, truth be told, it has been alive in me for many, many months; indeed, for years. It contains a secret that each of you must discover for yourself—what it feels like to come alive in someone else's mind, in someone else's heart. A secret I, the author of this book, intend to share with you as it has been shared with me: the secret of dreaming a new life into the world.

Whether that life is a book, or a business, or a new relationship doesn't really matter.

Whatever it becomes is a product of your imagination and your heart and your willingness to let go. Once you've done your part, you can settle back and wait to see what happens.

Oh, and did I mention love?

This book is a product of love. It is my gift to you, worthy reader, if you wish to know the truth about starting your own business. That you are doing it for the right reason does not have to be true. (It rarely is true!) Your desire is enough. Reading this book will be fueled by your desire, just as writing it was fueled by mine.

As you read this book, it will begin to pick up heat from your imagination, and it will become a Story you don't dare put down until you've finished it. This book is a Great Story! And now you are reading it, and my work is done. Your desire is enough, just as my desire was. This is a book about desire. The love of what you are feeling right now, *deep* down in your heart.

There is a secret waiting for you in this book. It's called "the Dreaming Room!"

Enjoy it! Savor it! Eat it up for breakfast, lunch, and dinner!

Good Dreaming!

Michael E. Gerber
Chief Dreamer
In the Dreaming Room
Carlsbad, California
January 1, 2008

# INTRODUCTION

> For once you are going to hear a dream, a dream that I
> have made sound . . . I dreamt all this: never could my
> poor head have invented such a thing purposely.
>
> —Richard Wagner

Over the past thirty years, I have worked intensively on the subject of entrepreneurship with tens of thousands of owners of small, medium, and large companies around the world trying to discover why people start companies, why so few succeed, what those that do succeed have in common, and what lessons others can learn from the dialogue I've been engaged in with these owners.

During that time I have recorded my findings in seven *E-Myth* books, all of which speak about the general conclusion I have reached in the process. That people who start a business are not the entrepreneurs we all believe them to be, but are what I have come to call "technicians suffering from an entrepreneurial seizure."

Thus, in the titles of my books, such as *The E-Myth: Why Most Small Businesses Don't Work and What to Do About It, E-Myth* stands for the "entrepreneurial myth," the end product of which is most often a business and life disaster.

The E-Myth says that technicians suffering from an entrepreneurial seizure believe that because they understand how to do the work of the business they intend to start, they are automatically gifted with an understanding about how to build and grow a business that does that work.

In my *E-Myth* books, I call that "the Fatal Assumption."

Fatal, because most small businesses that start that way, fail that way.

By believing that running a business is all about work, most small businesses don't work; the people who start, run, and attempt to succeed in them, do work hard but fail.

And, as the E-Myth says, most businesses and the people who start them fail because they are doing the wrong work. I call this work "doing it, doing it, doing it." The work of *being* the business, rather than *building* a business.

After teaching, coaching, training, and mentoring over 60,000 small business clients in the E-Myth methods, mind-set, and E-Myth process for changing that condition into one that works, I have discovered that everything we have taught our clients at E-Myth, while essential for growing a business once you've begun it, isn't nearly essential enough. What happens in a small and growing business *after* it's been started is only one small piece of the puzzle. It's what happens *before* one starts a business that's the key, and most essential, ingredient to business success.

The realization that I've come to is that the true start-up of a business is what happens before you start up.

It's what I have come to call, in this book and in the work I am currently doing in the Dreaming Room, "the Start-Up Is You."

## THE START-UP IS YOU

Yes, the start-up is you and nothing but you. For you to be successful at creating an entrepreneurial company, something quintessential has to occur inside of you before you open your business's doors, something I call the Moment of Inspiration, or that "sudden seeing."

The sudden seeing is the epiphany that happens when in

one inscrutable, revelatory instant, the world reveals its secrets to you.

That is a rare and indelible moment indeed. It is there in that lucid moment of clarity that the entrepreneur is provided with a rare glimpse inside a mystery, which is what a business is. It is a mystery in which people, processes, systems, ideas and facts, customers, investors, technology, and an overriding single-minded purpose come together to produce an original result that people love to produce inside the company and that people love to buy outside of the company. The result is both economic and experiential—both emotionally and pragmatically compelling. It is a result worthy of having spent a lot of time, money, imagination, and energy to produce.

All of this is begun in the mind, heart, and imagination of an entrepreneur before anything else happens. All of this is begun through a process that usually comes about through an accident, an interaction, a confluence of forces no one intended, but that moved the momentum of the entrepreneur's fertile imagination to pick up and take notice, and then to pursue whatever impression came to his or her attention to discover where that momentum was going.

All of that and more is what this book is about.

It's about awakening the entrepreneur in you. It's about stimulating a clear understanding in you about what truly artful, effective, dedicated entrepreneurs do that moves them and the business products they invent beyond all the rest of us.

Ultimately, though, it's about being personally invited into the Dreaming Room, where new businesses, much like books, are born.

The first step in the Dreaming Room is the Introduction. You are there now. The sign at the entrance says, "Welcome to the Dreaming Room."

I hope you have your wits about you. I hope that your shirt is sweatproof, that you're not afraid of being denied entry, or of being let out should you somehow be allowed in. I hope you have a good sense of humor and that your inner child doesn't feel too threatened by someone like me, who most often doesn't have one.

I hope you're really serious about this adventure we're about to go on together, and that you won't hold me responsible if you come out burned, if you lose your nerve, if you give up on becoming an entrepreneur entirely, and are glad you've still got a job and a loving wife or husband to go home to. I hope all that and more, dear reader, because this is going to be hard work. Sometimes you'll enjoy it. You'll have fun. Other times you won't enjoy it—it simply won't be fun.

However, even when you're not having fun, I can promise you that you will be making progress toward a significant goal.

I can promise you something else, too: This book will not insult your intelligence with stories about little engines that could. It won't provide you with cute little metaphors about losing and winning. Nor will it stimulate you with success stories that never really happened except in the minds of the ones who created them.

You are not a child, so you and I should have some strange sort of fun as we lock the door behind us and beat the imaginary drum together, calling forth the wizards, the angels, the shamans who make magic seem like no difficult thing even though, for the rest of us, it is still magic after all. And it is one huge mother of a difficult thing when you don't know where your next meal is coming from.

At least that's what it has been like for me over the seventy years of my life, as I found it difficult oftentimes just to breathe, let alone create miracles called *businesses*.

Are you still with me? Do you want to hear more?

Then hear this: To create a miracle company, or a miracle life, takes a magnificent sense of the surreal. You have to be ready to see things that fly away faster than a thought, and capture them in your lens without skipping a beat.

The Dreaming Room is serious, serious work.

It's a challenge to you, the reader, and a promise, if you accept my challenge . . . that we will tussle and wrestle and hammerlock each other, we will move into it with the most forceful language I can muster, to engage the mind in the electricity of what happens when serious, serious folks take on the serious, serious challenge of creating an enormous, mind-boggling Idea, a stunningly original company, that looks like nothing you or anyone else you know has ever seen or done before.

And especially because the treacherously depressing fact is that most will fail.

Yes, that's the humbling fact of it all. That entrepreneurs, even the very best of us, will rise up, be possessed by some strange delirium of inspired thought, rise up some more, and then start running, thinking all the time, "This is it! By God, this is it!" only to discover as we're rounding the corner, that we're about to run into a wall! There's no denying it. It's a wall, and *smack*, too late! It's a hit!

That's where the Dreaming Room begins, and stops, and begins again—in the face of the wall. *Pow!* You're down for the count, and you've started to get up. Now what? What happens when you've dusted yourself off? That's the question the Dreaming Room poses: Now what? Now where do we go? Now what's the next Big Idea waiting in the hopper of your suddenly humbled imagination? Are you ready to do that once more? Are you? Are you seriously ready to try again?

Well, let's go at it.

Welcome to the Dreaming Room.

Come Dream with me.

PART ONE

# THE
# PREPARATION

# 1

# A Conversation with My Mother Leads to the Dreaming Room

*All the influences were lined up waiting for me.*
*I was born and there they were to form me,*
*which is why I tell you more of them than of myself.*

—Saul Bellow, *The Adventures of Augie March*

My mother is ninety-six, lives an active life, looks to be no more than sixty, and has a wonderful sense of humor about it all. "One day I won't be here," she says with a twinkle in her eye, "but don't give me up for dead yet!"

My mother loves to talk, and she loves it even more when I talk. She loves it when I visit her and share my life with her. She eats up all my stories when I tell them, which I usually don't because I can't bear to hear them since I'm living them. She has read every one of my seven books, which amazes me since she has no interest in business.

She puts it this way: "Your books are you, Michael, and I get to experience you when I read what you've written. I love your books," she says, her eyes going deep when she says it, "because I love *you*. You're a remarkable man, Michael. I know I'm your mother, and that's what mothers are supposed to say and feel, but, please know that I mean it; even if I weren't your mother, you are a remarkable man." It's always difficult for me to hear that when my mother says that because I don't feel like a remarkable man. I just feel like me, which is not remarkable. But don't we all feel that way?

So, in 2005, my mother asked me, "So, what's going on in your life, Michael?"

"I'm feeling lost, Mom," I said. "I'm sixty-nine years old and I'm feeling like I used to feel when I was a kid. I don't know who I am anymore, or where I'm going. I feel disconnected from my company and disconnected from myself. I want to do something new but I don't know what. I feel at a loss, disconnected from the past and the future, and not doing very well in the present, either. I don't even know how to say it."

My mother smiled, "Michael, if there's one thing I know about you, you're never at a loss for words! Tell me what you would tell me if you *did* know how to say it." She sat there with that lovely enigmatic smile of hers.

"It's just that, for the past twenty-nine years, I have been so immersed in creating my life, my books, my company, the world I live in, the speaking—all of it. It's been my passion. And while it's been difficult at times, it's also been extraordinary beyond belief. I have been someone, have done something that few people have ever done, have come to this place in my life knowing that I've had a positive impact on millions of people in the world, and yet . . ."

I paused, feeling that I was missing the point somehow, but continued to push through it.

"Oh, God, that's not really it, Mom; it's something much less obvious. It's that, yes, all that is true, but at the heart of it something is missing in all of it. I have been so consumed with the path I was on I stopped looking at where it was taking me. It's like the path became the purpose. But the path I was on . . . still am on . . . is simply that, one path among many. And it could have been a million different paths, had I paid attention somewhere along the way; it could have been anything. I could have done anything, other than what I have done. And I'm feeling the loss of the many paths not chosen because of the one I did take. I have committed myself to becoming 'Mr. E-Myth' and I don't know how to disengage from him now that he's become such a reality to so many people, and to me. I guess what I'm saying is that I need to find a new path, and, at sixty-nine, I feel foolish and lost because I don't know how, or even why, I want to do it."

My mother said, "Michael, pardon me if I don't take what you've said seriously. You've never been at a loss for ideas. You're one of the most imaginative people I know. So, we both know it's not that you can't figure out what to do. It's that somehow you're not really dealing with the problem. Somehow you're avoiding what's really eating at you. What is it? What's making you feel so off?"

I suddenly knew what it was. It came to me so quickly, so immediately, so sharply, and clearly, that I was amazed I hadn't seen it until that minute.

"I'm afraid, Mom. I'm afraid to start something brand-new. I'm afraid that I won't have what it took me to start E-Myth all those years ago. That I could actually create something new that is as powerful as E-Myth has been. I'm afraid I'm too old, too used up, too stuck in my E-Myth rut. And, at the same time, I'm afraid to let go of E-Myth for fear that all the work I've done, all the life I've put in it, will simply lose force and die a slow and ugly death. I'm afraid that the people I've left it to won't cherish it as I do. Won't respect it as I respect it. Won't honor it the way it deserves to be honored. And, if that happens, then none of what I've done will really matter. It will end up being just a book. One book among millions of books, but what it has done for tens of thousands of people will stop. And I would hate that."

My mother had not stopped smiling during my rant, but her smile softened to a sadness, which was reflected in her pale eyes as she looked at me.

"Michael, I feel your pain. I do. I can only imagine how difficult it would be to have to start all over again. But, of course, you don't have to. You could do anything you wish to do now. The only reason you feel so conflicted is because you're coming awake to energy in you, the same energy that has been bubbling and bursting and playing inside of you ever since you were a little boy. Just let it, Michael. Stop thinking. Just let it bubble and burst and play inside you, and see what happens. It's telling you something. It's telling you that that little boy I love so much is just aching to come out. He's the one who is making such a ruckus in you. He's the one who created the E-Myth when everyone told you that you were crazy. He's the one who still wants to play, no matter what time it is, no matter what anybody has to say. Michael, you've always been like that. Let go, and let it do what it does. I have a feeling everything will change. It feels like it's time for something new to come into your life, Michael," my beautiful mother said. "Isn't that exciting?"

It was exactly at that moment when "In the Dreaming Room" was born in earnest: when an entirely new phase of my life began; when my inner entrepreneur was awakened, and a flood of new impressions catapulted me out of my lethargy and drew me to places I had never been before; when the inventor in me woke up and thought, "I'm awake!"

This was really good! It had been so many years since I had felt like this. As the entrepreneur within me began to see and feel and think. As the entrepreneur within me began to say, "What if?" and "Why not?" and "Why doesn't anyone know about that?"

All of that happened in the few weeks following my conversation with my mother, and it was more intensive work than I had done in the previous thirty years. But, in the thirty years prior to this epiphany—this moment of seeing clearly, this awakening of the entrepreneur within me—I had done everything I needed to do to prepare me to write this book. I was now ready to take millions of people—those who want to wake up the entrepreneur within them and discover an independent life—closer to their dreams than I had ever believed I could.

That is what this book is about. It's that process, the awakening, that I want to describe to you.

Before I do that, let me set the rules of the game straight. The rules for playing the Game of the New Entrepreneur. The rules for inventing a new life out of nothing other than the most delightful, most remarkable and miraculous thing of all . . . your imagination.

Let's look at the Five Realities of the Entrepreneur.

# 2

## The Five Realities
## of the Entrepreneur

I believe there are two ways to look at a blank sheet of
paper. The first way is that the blank sheet is the
most frightening thing in the world because you
have to put down the first mark and figure out what
to do with it. The other way is to look at it and say, "Wow,
I've got another blank piece of paper. This is the greatest
opportunity in the world because I can now let my
imagination fly in any direction and I can create whole
new things." I have spent a good part of my life convincing
people that the blank sheet is the greatest opportunity
in the world and is not frightening at all.

—Marty Sklar, Executive Vice President/Imagineering
Ambassador, Walt Disney Imagineering

### REALITY #1

**An entrepreneur is an inventor**, although few inventors are entrepreneurs. An inventor sees the world through alert, wide-open eyes. An inventor lives asking the question, "What's missing in this picture?" and then answers it by inventing the missing piece that makes the picture whole. He can't help himself, it's just what he is called to do. What an entrepreneur does next, however, is what makes the difference between him and all other inventors.

An entrepreneur invents new businesses. All other inventors invent new products. To the entrepreneur, the business he or she invents *is* a product, a unique product that stands out in a world of ordinary business products and, through its uniqueness, captures the attention and imagination of the people for whom it was invented: its customer, its employees, its suppliers, and its lenders and investors.

To the degree a business does not achieve that uniqueness, that originality, from the very beginning, it is not an invention. To the degree a business is not an invention, it is not an entrepreneurial business. While being an entrepreneurial business is not a guarantee of success, failing to be an entrepreneurial business is a guarantee of failure.

## REALITY #2

**Entrepreneurs do not *buy* business opportunities; they *create* them.** While business opportunities such as franchises are more likely to guarantee the success of the person who buys them, they are only successful to the degree the buyer suppresses his or her inclination to invent—suppresses his or her entrepreneurial passion. Therefore, entrepreneurs who buy business opportunities are doomed to disappointment, no matter how successful the business is. The passion of the entrepreneur is not to run a successful business—not to run a business someone else invented—but to invent a unique business that becomes successful.

Business opportunities are invented for technicians or managers to run who have no aspiration to be entrepreneurs—who have no aspiration to create anything of their own other than a successful job. Ninety-nine percent of business opportunities are actually jobs for the people who buy them. They may be better jobs (most actually aren't!) than the ones the buyers had before, but they are still jobs, not true business opportunities. A true business opportunity is the one that an entrepreneur invents to grow him or herself. Not to work in, but to work on. That's the work of an entrepreneur.

## REALITY #3

**Invention is contagious.** People love to experience an original business idea that has been successfully manifested in the world. So, the entrepreneur's passion comes not only from inventing a new business but also from basking in the delight of other people as they gladly experience his or her invention. The entrepreneur, in this sense, is no different from a performer whose love for what he or she does is dramatically increased by the enthusiastic response from the audience.

For the entrepreneur, there is nothing more satisfying than when the audience applauds the performance. Every customer who buys from the entrepreneur's business and then comes back for more is applauding the entrepreneur's originality, brilliance, and successful performance. The entrepreneur loves accolades, lives for the successful manifestation of the invention, and finds joy only when the audience and the business truly come together as originally envisioned.

Once the business has achieved that level of success, sustaining it becomes the primary focus of the entrepreneur. The more significant the invention, the easier it is to sustain its success. The less significant the invention, the more difficult it is to sustain its success.

## REALITY #4

**To an entrepreneur, the success of the invention—the business—is measured by growth.** The faster the business grows, the more successful is the invention. The slower the business grows, the less successful is the invention. To an entrepreneur, *slow* growth or *no* growth is death. To be caught up in a slow- or no-growth business is to be doomed to show up every day to perform in a show nobody enjoys.

On Broadway, shows that nobody enjoys close quickly. Businesses that nobody enjoys should close quickly so that everyone can go out looking for an experience they love.

Unfortunately, most businesses don't close soon enough. They just linger on and on and on, surviving as best they can. Entrepreneurs should never create a business simply because it can survive. To do so would be to commit oneself to daily dying. Entrepreneurs create businesses that thrive. To the entrepreneur, "There's no business like show business!" It's always, "Let's get on with the show!"

## REALITY #5

*Everyone* possesses the ability to be an entrepreneur—to invent, to conceive of a great idea for a new business, and to create an original business based upon a simple but explosive idea. For some of us it may take longer to develop that ability, it may take more work. For others it may take little more than the awareness of what differentiates the entrepreneur from the manager and the technician to set off a flood of entrepreneurial excitement. In either case, however, it is necessary for each of us to know that learning to invent, to create, to conceive of an original business is both a process of discovery and the development of the patience necessary to sustain one's interest while developing one's skill.

Developing one's entrepreneurial skill calls for practice. That does not mean that you have to start a business to develop that skill—not at first, in any case. It simply means you have to develop the practice of creating new ideas for a business, again and again, just as all inventors do. All that's required is a blank piece of paper and beginner's mind. All that's required is the interest to begin.

Entrepreneurs are made, not born. There is no corner on creativity. There is simply the desire to express it. Once that desire appears, you can be assured that you have awakened the entrepreneur within. The very presence of that desire means that the entrepreneur is up and dreaming.

Before we can begin the process in earnest, you must understand that these five realities are defined and expressed by four dimensions of the entrepreneurial personality: the Dreamer, the Thinker, the Storyteller, and the Leader. Because it is the way entrepreneurs function in the real world that enables them to pursue untold business opportunities and then manifest their abilities to create a successful venture or successful ventures.

# 3

# The Four Dimensions of the Entrepreneurial Personality

It is only when the mind is free from the old that it
meets everything anew, and in that there is joy.

—J. Krishnamurti, *The First and Last Freedom*

There are four dimensions of the entrepreneurial personality
that come into play in the creation of a new venture: the
Dreamer, the Thinker, the Storyteller, and the Leader. It's important
to get a better understanding of the role each plays in the conception
of an enterprise.

## THE DREAMER

Surprisingly, the Dreamer is the least known and understood personality within the entrepreneur. You would think it would be exactly the opposite. Everyone knows that entrepreneurs dream, but few people truly know what it means to dream. They think of dreaming as daydreaming, as wishful thinking.

Dr. Martin Luther King, Jr., had a clear dream, but few of us can be said to "have a dream of our own"; one that moves us, consumes us, keeps us awake at night, a dream as big to us as Dr. King's dream was to him. Is there a Dreamer in you who will have an epiphany when the Purpose is suddenly revealed as *your* Purpose, as the one thing you were brought here on this earth to fulfill?

Who is that Dreamer—that one inside you—who is so inspired, so completely aroused, that there is no question that you are going to do this? The only question is, "When and how?"

Who is that Dreamer in the center of you? Not the one who dreams about getting a new home, or moving to Hawaii, or becoming a millionaire, or finding the perfect mate.

I'm referring to the other one. This Dreamer lives at the center of the entrepreneur's heart. Without this Dreamer, the entrepreneur would have no real life, and would get busy with life's toys to eradicate, or at least muffle, the pain that comes from having given up on the possibilities. This Dreamer pictures a life in which little dreams are distractions rather than substance. This Dreamer stands on the mountaintop of imagination, and creates dreams where there are none at all. This Dreamer's Dream comes to us in the light, yet we avoid looking directly into it for fear we will not be big enough to bear it.

## THE THINKER

The Thinker is the Dreamer's most important companion, his most important ally. He listens carefully to the Dreamer's thoughts, and knows that without the special role he plays in the manifestation of the Dreamer's *vision*, the Dreamer would be lost.

The Thinker is the one who thinks "how" in relation to the Dreamer's extreme "what." The Thinker asks the questions essential to formulating the business model—the form the Dream will take visually, emotionally, functionally, and financially—as well as the impact the Dream will have on its customers, its investors, its employees, its suppliers, and its strategic partners.

What is unique about the Venture? What will be delivered? How will it be delivered? What are the core operating assumptions of the Venture? What problem is it intended to solve, and how will that problem be solved? Will it be solved cost effectively?

The Thinker, however, is not the devil's advocate in his relationship with the Dreamer. Rather, the Thinker's role is to help the Dreamer fulfill the Dream in ways the Dreamer might not have anticipated. The objective is to empower the right-brained genius of the Dreamer by melding it with the left-brained genius of the Thinker.

When the Dreamer finally consults with the Thinker, the goal is to help make the Dream even more compelling and viable. The Dreamer's requests are, "Show me the financial advantages of doing business this way, the functional advantages of doing business this way, the marketing advantages of doing business this way, and the brand advantages of doing business this way. Is there another way we could accomplish my objectives and fulfill my dream that I'm not aware of?"

The Thinker revels in putting the puzzle together in a way that supports his right-brained self. The outcome of the Thinker's participation in the entrepreneurial process is a white paper that spells out in great specificity the argument for proceeding toward the actual planning and design stage of the Venture being dreamed into being.

## THE STORYTELLER

The Storyteller could be called by his other name, the Performer. He is the one who evokes excitement when the Dream is conveyed to other people. The Storyteller knows that without a compelling story, no Dream would become a reality in the world of ordinary people in which the Dream is intended to manifest itself as a striking reality. The Storyteller knows that without a compelling story, no Dream would ever become a reality. The Storyteller digs deeply into the Dreamer's Vision and the Thinker's formulation of that Vision, and looks for the creative arc that lies at the heart of every great story.

The Storyteller begins to "speak" the Dream, to "sing" the Story, to test its sound as she tells it to many, many people on all ends of the spectrum. They may be people in the industry, people in other industries, people who could be customers, people who could be managers, people who are simply great audiences and love a good story. They may be people the Storyteller knows or might just have met.

The Storyteller cannot test his reality without people. People determine if the Story either rings true or rings hollow. To the Storyteller, a great story is the essence of life. To the Dreamer and the Thinker, the Storyteller is the means through which they find voice.

## THE LEADER

The Leader is the one who assumes responsibility for moving the Dream forward, takes accountability for fulfilling the Dream, for knowing where he is going, how he is going to get there, when he's going to get there, and what the venture will look like when it gets there. The Leader takes on the Vision and the formulation of the enterprise. The Leader knows the Story, buys the Story, lives the Story, is committed to the Story, and tells the Story in concrete terms that are evidence of the fact that the Story is more than just a story but rather a tangible reality that can be lived and experienced.

The Leader possesses the passion of the Dreamer, the intellect of the Thinker, and the joy of the Storyteller. The Leader knows that all big things are the product of small things done very, very well.

The Leader possesses the five essential skills of concentration, discrimination, organization, innovation, and communication, through which all great things are made real in the world. To the degree in which the Leader is deficient in any or all of those skills, he makes it a point to develop his or her capability in each, knowing that his mission, to be realized, will demand more of him or her than he imagines at the outset, and, like the good Boy or Girl Scout, the Leader is constantly aware of the possibility that he or she may not be prepared and ready or able to do his very best. To be prepared is the hallmark of a worthy Leader, no matter how silly that might sound to him or her when it is said.

He also knows that once the Dreamer and the Thinker and the Storyteller have created the platform upon which the Leader will stand, the entire success of the Venture rests squarely on his or her shoulders. That he has bought the Dream, agreed with the logic of it, internalized the Story is insufficient for the Dream to become a successful reality; when all is said and done, the Leader must execute it to the best of his or her ability and beyond. All things finally rest upon the Leader. There is no escaping the Leader's overriding accountability if the Dream is to become a reality.

■

So, now we begin the process that every entrepreneur takes to invent, conceive, articulate, and build a new venture, whether he or she knows it or not. And that's finally the true point of this book: to describe via experience exactly what the entrepreneurial process feels like, looks like, when one goes through it. What follows is not just my experience, it is the aggregate of countless thousands of entrepreneurs' experiences as they Dream about, Think about, Tell a Story about, and Lead out a venture they first conceived in their mind.

It is my hope that as you follow me step by step you will come to understand not only the process, but also the people within you who are going to do the inventing. Your Dreamer. Your Thinker. Your Storyteller. Your Leader.

They are extraordinary persons all.

Remember this as you move forward: There is nothing set in this process. Nothing limiting at all. It is a product of one man's imagination: mine. It has shown itself to be stunningly effective with many hundreds of Dreamers from my Dreaming Rooms, and many tens of thousands of entrepreneurs who preceded them, as well as many millions to follow. Be grateful for their spirit. Be thankful for their courage. Be respectful of their daring. And be stimulated by their willingness to risk everything for a simple idea. It is that which this book has as its Mission: to awaken the entrepreneur within you to create your own footprints in the fresh earth of time. I am with you.

# PART TWO

# THE DREAMER

## AND

# THE DREAM

# 4

# The Awakening

The awakening to the mystery of life is a revolutionary
event; in it an old world is destroyed so that a new and
better one may take its place, and all things are affected by
the change. We ourselves have become mysterious
strangers in our own eyes and tremblingly we ask ourselves
who we are, whence we came, whither we are bound. Are
we the being who is called by our name, whom we thought
we knew so well in the past? Are we the form we see in the
mirror, our body, offspring of our parents? Who, then, is it
that feels and thinks within us, that wills and struggles,
plans and dreams, that can oppose and control this
physical body which we thought to be ourselves? We wake
up to realize that we have never known ourselves, that we
have lived as in a blind dream of ceaseless activity in
which there was never a moment of self recollection.

—J. J. Van Der Leeuw, *The Conquest of Illusion*

When I first came to my true entrepreneurial calling, I was on
my way to doing something else.

I had just finished working side by side with a master carpenter
who taught me everything I needed to know about framing a house.
It was a key experience for me, a course in how to truly master a skill.
Previous such courses had been learning to play the saxophone, from
the age nine to age seventeen, with a master saxophone teacher; learn-

ing how to sell encyclopedias in my early twenties with a master sales-man; and learning why I failed in my attempts to do the Gurdjieff work with someone who I am certain also failed it. (I buried all my Gurdjieff-related books in the backyard of my home twelve years later, with a fitting ceremony accompanied by lit candles, to finally end that chapter in my life.) And for those of you who've never heard of Gurdjieff, well, be glad that his teachings have happily run their course.

Fortunately for you, this is not one of those books.

This book, unlike many, is devoted to the truth gleaned from my personal and very direct experience over thirty years of dogged pur-suit of the impossible, which, in my life, meant how to produce an extremely practical result on a massive scale, without giving up my soul while doing it. (One other book that comes immediately to mind is *The Tracker* by Tom Brown, Jr. Look it up. It will blow your mind.)

On with the story. In mid-1975, I had stopped over to visit a friend of mine, Arnie West (not his real name), to rest and to talk before setting out on my way to Mendocino County, California, where I envisioned buying a small ranch and becoming a contractor. I planned to build homes, and live the life of woods, fields, streams— writing, dreaming, doing good things. Whatever those good things would be, I had no idea.

It just felt good to dream about the idyllic life, the life of produc-tivity, the life with horses perhaps, with dogs and cats, with chickens and ducks and sheep and whatever else the good life had in store for me.

I loved to dream. My mind would fly away at a moment's notice, or, even without notice. I would be dreaming about one thing at one moment, then begin to dream about another thing at another moment without a pause in between.

There was no plan to it—no method, no intention, no practice, no theme, other than the theme that my mind made up in the moment. No matter how disorganized I now know it to be, at the time there was a distinct sense of self in it all.

I was completely caught up with the enthusiasm of what lay before me, the thrill of whatever came up.

It was in that state that I stopped to visit my friend, Arnie West, in Belmont, California. That is when Arnie invited me to join him to call on his client nearby.

■

I have written about this meeting with Arnie's client in my previous books, but let me embellish it a bit for you, whether you've read them or not.

I repeat it here, because this meeting, as innocuous as it appeared when Arnie first suggested it to me, was to become the seminal event of my life.

It was when *the Awakening* occurred.

In this meeting, everything I had learned and done came to-gether—my saxophone lessons, my sales lessons, my Gurdjieff les-sons, my carpentry lessons, my experience being a saxophone player, a salesman, a sales manager, a carpenter, a hopeless romantic, as well as a philosopher, a dreamer, a poet—all of that and more, came with me to that first meeting.

Arnie asked me to take a look at his client's business to see why he wasn't converting the leads Arnie's advertising was creating for him. I told Arnie I didn't know anything about business. He said it didn't matter; I knew all that I needed to know. With that encouragement, and nothing to lose, we arrived at his client's office with a few min-utes to spare. His client's name was Bob, and he was seated at his desk in a small corner office when we arrived, busy working with a mound of papers stacked in obsessively neat piles.

Arnie introduced us and then said, "I have some things to do. I'll be back in an hour. Why don't you two get to know each other?" Then, without another word, he abruptly left the office with Bob and me looking at each other wondering who was going to speak first.

Bob broke the silence by asking me what I knew about his business. I answered, "Nothing, Bob."

Bob looked a bit surprised. "Well, what do you know about my products?"

"Less than I know about your business, Bob."

Now Bob looked truly uncomfortable. "Well, if you don't know anything about my business, and you don't know anything about my products, how can you help me?"

"I haven't the foggiest idea, Bob, but Arnie thinks I can, and you like Arnie and I like Arnie, so let's see what happens. We've got an hour to kill."

And with that, I began to do the only thing that made sense to me at the time. I began to ask Bob questions. Questions about his business, about his products, and about what was working and what didn't seem to be.

I started that hour with two basic assumptions that I knew with certainty to be true. First, that I didn't know anything about business. And second, because Bob owned a business—a high-tech business to boot—he *did* know something about business.

By the time that hour went by, both of my assumptions were turned on their ear.

First, I discovered that I did know something about business. I knew that selling is a system. I had learned that so very well from my sales master. "This is how you do it" became second nature to me. Of course, that was equally true with my saxophone master and my Gurdjieff master and my carpenter master as well. All of my masters lived by one credo: that there was a specific way to do what they were teaching me to do, and my only job was to master that way. Their way. The only way, as far as each of them was concerned.

The second assumption fell apart as quickly as the first one did. I was astonished to discover that Bob didn't know that selling was a system, nor did he seem to know that *everything* having to do with the operation of his business was a system. And that, I deduced in my naïveté, but which proved itself to be remarkably accurate in time, was why he was experiencing so many problems.

As the hour came to a close, I felt myself close to bursting. The excitement I felt was palpable. The rush of energy was overwhelming. I had just entered a completely new world, and that world was saying, "You've found it, Michael. You've found your true calling! Welcome to the rest of your life."

■

Yes, that was my first Awakening. My second Awakening occurred when my ninety-four-year-old mother told me it was time to create a new life. That was in late spring 2005, when I was sixty-nine years old—thirty years after my first Awakening in 1975.

This is important to understand. The Awakening I'm describing is the flashpoint where the entrepreneur within comes awake with the sudden seeing of an opportunity that he had never seen before.

It's as if he were hibernating until that auspicious moment, waiting silently for something to occur, when, for reasons unknown to him, something says, "Wake up!" and he does, hungry as a bear coming out of a long winter's sleep to eat his fill of all these extraordinary and luscious new foods that are beckoning him.

There is no sensation I know of that matches it. That sudden seeing. That awakening to an idea that comes fully into view, uninvited, unanticipated, calling you out into the glare of that burning, joyous light outside. And all the rest of me steps aside, when he comes forward, when the entrepreneur within me awakens and takes his place in my life. He awakens to create. He awakens to be joyous. He awakens in me with such a sudden, overwhelming, and delightful force as to make the rest of me feel like *it* was asleep. And the joy and exhilaration in challenge, which is so foreign to my ordinary life, also wake up. And the thrill of imagination, which is also foreign to the rest of my ordinary, oh so ordinary, life also wakes up with him, the entrepreneur within me.

# STOP

## AND

# FOCUS

## The Awakening

*We have come to that wonderful point in your life where you have been invited to go down an exciting path, either forward from where you are now, or down a completely new path. A path you haven't trod upon before.*

*That path and the invitation it extends to you are both exciting and threatening. Exciting because you have been provided with an unanticipated fork in the road of your life that is speaking to you in a language you are unaccustomed to. It's not exactly a foreign language, but it is a language that speaks to you differently from the language you are accustomed to. It is speaking to you in the voice of opportunity. It is a language that promises to bring you something you have been longing for, but haven't pursued, because it threatens to take you away from everything that has led you up to this point in your life. It is threatening, this new path of opportunity, because the path is leading to the unknown. We see our normal life, and the future extension of it, as predictable. We see our epiphany, this moment of awakening, as new and unpredictable. Because of all that, this exact moment in your life is rich with meaning. Stop and savor it. Pause before you choose one path or the other. Focus your mind on what this feels like, what this means to you. Stop and focus on the tug*

*(continued)*

*inside to go one way or the other. You are in the midst of your awakening. The entrepreneur within you is speaking to you. He or she is saying that this moment is more important than you can possibly imagine, no matter what you choose to do. Stop. Focus. Listen. Feel.*

# 5

# The Realization

The foremost step in decoding the material world
is seeing past the material itself.

—Todd Siler, *Breaking the Mind Barrier*

I couldn't wait for Arnie to return. I needed to share with somebody what had just happened. I waited outside Bob's office, shifting excitedly from foot to foot.

I had just sold Bob my services to help him build his selling system.

We didn't arrive at a price for my services, because I didn't know what they were worth. I told Bob that Arnie would work that out with him. After all, he was Arnie's client. And what I was about to do was to provide Bob with a capability that Arnie should be providing.

After talking to Bob it was immediately apparent to me that despite the fact that Arnie thought he was in the advertising business, he was really in the sales business, only Arnie didn't know it. Bob didn't want advertising. He wanted sales. And Arnie wasn't giving him what he wanted. I wondered if Arnie had ever thought about his business that way—that the service I was about to provide Bob was really an extension of what Arnie already did. A necessary extension, as a matter of fact.

Understand, none of that went through my mind as I was talking to Bob, but it was running through my mind now like a freight train at full speed. My mind was suddenly brimming with opportunity. Wow, Arnie could offer this service—the development of selling systems—to every one of his advertising clients. If every one of his clients knew as little as Bob did about sales, Arnie's advertising firm could become a unique firm in its field. Did Arnie know that when he asked me to meet with Bob? Was that Arnie's intention all along? Did Arnie know what he was getting me into?

"But, wait a minute," I thought to myself. "Everybody in the advertising business did know what I just found out." How could they not? It was so obvious. "For that matter," I thought, "Bob is a really intelligent guy. How could he not know what I just witnessed?" Somebody in this mysterious world of business and high technology and advertising must know what I just found out.

Just then Arnie drove up. I got into his car and I enthusiastically poured out my discovery to him. I swear, if Bob looked surprised and then concerned as I told him that I didn't know anything about his business or his products, Arnie looked practically mortified! "You what?" he said to me. "You *sold* him your *services*? *What* services?" he asked, as if I had just told him I had sold his house.

"Hell, I don't know what to call it, Arnie. I've never done this before . . . But I told him I'd build him a selling system like the one I used when selling encyclopedias."

"Are you out of your mind, Michael?" Arnie asked me. "What do you know about Bob's business, or his products, or his customers, or how to sell them?"

"Arnie," I responded, "that's what *I* said before we went on this little journey. You told me I knew all I needed to know. And the truth is, I do."

■

Fast-forward thirty years: it was time for me to create in the summer of 2005, and I knew it to be true. I knew that I would begin to do something with my newly found free time just as I did when I met Bob all those years before, and the entrepreneur within me woke up for the first time. And remarkably, although I was now sixty-nine, not thirty-nine, the entrepreneur within me was no older, no less excited, no less thrilled, than he had been all those years before.

What *was* different this time was that I had been completely un-aware that the entrepreneur within me had gone to sleep! I thought he was awake! Unlike 1975, by the summer of 2005 I had spent the past thirty years writing about entrepreneurship, thinking about en-trepreneurship, speaking about entrepreneurship, *being* an entrepre-neur in my own company. My God, I had even become regarded as a thought leader in entrepreneurship the world over. And yet, here I was, suddenly experiencing entrepreneurship for what seemed like the very first time in close to thirty years, at the age of sixty-nine! "How could that be?" I wondered. "How could I have been so asleep? What have I been doing all these years, if not entrepreneurship?"

The answer came to me immediately. I was being a manager and a technician just like my clients were. "Oh, yes, you are, Michael," I told myself. And even as I said it I knew it to be true. I knew that the Awakening I was experiencing was as rare and as sacred a thing as any person could experience. One is either ready for it or not—that in-sight, that amazing prescient realization, that, as I call it, sudden seeing. When it comes up roaring—when the sudden joyous light breaks through the thick clouds of your unknowing—be available, be open to it.

That day, the Awakening came forth in me with a stunning, glowing, irresistible force. And the Dreaming Room was born just as the E-Myth had been born thirty years before it.

# STOP

## AND

# FOCUS

## *The Realization*

*This has happened to you before, this realization. Remember the times it has happened. Remember what you thought when it happened. Remember what you did when it happened. Write down all of these thoughts, remembrances, and the feelings they produced in you. Take a few moments to recall as much as you can about the realizations you have had when confronted by a sudden choice, an opportunity that suddenly spoke to you.*

*Isn't that how your life has been up to this point? A series of incidents in which someone or some experience or some circumstance spoke to you and invited you to go down a new path, and you responded enthusiastically, and you wanted with all of your being to do what had come to you, to pursue it, to take the leap? Or, you did exactly the opposite? Think back to all of those times and to what your response was.*

# 6

# The Negative Reaction

The greatest crisis of our lives is neither economic,
intellectual, nor even what we usually call religious. It is a
crisis of imagination. We get stuck on our paths because
we are unable to reimagine our lives differently from what
they are right now. We hold on desperately to the status
quo, afraid that if we let go, we will be swept away by
the torrential undercurrents of our emptiness.

—Marc Gafni, *The Mystery of Love*

The drive back to Arnie's was a memorable one. Arnie was
dumbfounded at how I could have put him and me in such a
ticklish situation. What was he supposed to say to Bob about what I
had promised to do for him?

Arnie saw this thing I had done as a problem. I saw it as the most
extraordinary opportunity that had ever come my way.

Arnie saw this thing as something that had to be fixed. I saw it as
something that I had to pursue with everything I had.

Arnie saw this thing as something that was fraught with difficulty,
that threatened to complicate his life, his business, his delicately bal-
anced relationship with his employees, with his clients. I saw this

thing as something that was rich with possibility, which had simplified my life.

Arnie became seriously confused. I became seriously focused.

Arnie saw this thing with the left side of his brain . . . the Thinker. I saw this thing with the right side of my brain . . . the Dreamer. Arnie's Thinker was repelled by this new, unmanageable, illogical situation. My Dreamer was entranced by this new, unlimited, compellingly exciting, and immeasurably vast situation. Arnie's Thinker lacked proof that I could do what I sold Bob, and was angry because he was being forced to deal with it. My Dreamer had all the proof it needed because he could see the successful conclusion of this. Even though he had never done it before, it had been done by somebody— his sales master—so why couldn't Bob and I do it?

Well, of course we could, my Dreamer saw. There was no logic needed to convince him of that. None at all. Or at least not the kind of logic that was causing Arnie so much difficulty.

The Dreamer doesn't need logic. The Dreamer defies logic. The Dreamer lives in a logic-free world. The Dreamer is logic's archenemy, even though the Dreamer knows that logic will have its time, will need to be rewarded, will need to be dealt with some time in the process, but no, not right now.

Right now, when the entrepreneur is just awakening, is the worst time of all for logic to rear its ugly head. "Keep the left brain at bay," says the knowing, right-brained being. He, the Thinker, who lives to think, will kill your dream as quickly as it comes to your fascinated, fascinating, right-brained mind.

■

Arnie persisted, no matter how enthusiastically I responded. "Michael, you don't know what these guys are like. When you promise results, they expect them. When you don't deliver the results you promise, there's hell to pay. That's why advertising agencies don't promise results. We can't promise them. Advertising is a crapshoot. Sometimes it works, and sometimes it doesn't. All we can do is try to produce results. And the only result we can try to produce is that we'll generate responses to our ads, that people will be stimulated to call our client, or to send in a request for more information. What you're promising is beyond comprehension. Sure, you can help Bob organize his response, but you can't promise that he'll use your 'system,' or, if he does, that it will work."

I was amazed at how negatively Arnie looked at the situation, which was a situation that I knew to be rich with possibilities. Then I realized, as though for the very first time, that Arnie had never really ever sold anything, other than his advertising services. But, in that case, his clients were only buying what he was selling . . . advertising services . . . They didn't expect him to deliver anything other than a method for reaching the customers they wanted to reach.

It was like Arnie was in the billboard business. You paint a billboard with the message you want to put forward, and you place the billboard in the highest-traffic area you can afford, and then wait, hoping that someone will respond to it. It's exactly what millions of advertisers do on the Internet today; they put up their website with the message they want to put out there, and then wait. Millions upon millions of messages, all sitting in cyberspace, waiting for someone to see them. Just waiting, little different than it was in the seventies as I was driving in the car with Arnie, amazed at the extraordinary realization I had just had, which was about to transform my life forever.

But, still, there was the sudden onslaught of doubt. After all, Arnie was right. In the world he lived in my idea was simply that—an idea.

Worse, it was an *uninformed* idea, the worst kind of idea one can have, according to the Thinker. An idea born out of—what? Enthusiasm? A beginner's excitement? An idea that came from a completely unrelated set of experiences, selling encyclopedias, playing the saxophone, building a house? Reading poetry, fiction, philosophy, works of the spiritual kind? What in the world did any of that have to do with converting leads for high-tech products into the sale of high-tech products? Or, even more, creating a selling system, which would also call for the creation of a selling training system, which would also call for the creation of a selling recruitment and hiring system, which would also call for the creation of a selling management system, which would also call for an order entry system and a client fulfillment system and a salesperson's time management system if the selling system were going to work.

And I suddenly had the overwhelming sensation that I was in this completely over my head! After all, what had I ever done to lead me to believe that I suddenly possessed the answer to Bob's sales problems? My God, Bob was an engineer; he had made it in a world I didn't even know existed before I walked into his office. He had successfully accumulated the money necessary to start a sophisticated business. What had I ever done? Nothing.

I was suddenly awash with embarrassment. A wave of heat flushed over my face. Who in the world was I to think that I held the key to Arnie's business, or anyone else's for that matter? The enthusiasm I was feeling just moments before completely left me. I was immediately ridden with shame for having come to the conclusions I had. To think that, the moment before, I had created in my mind an entirely new world for myself! Was I insane? Was I out of my mind? Did I honestly believe that I could transform Bob's business and, with it, my life?

■

It hit me about halfway through my first Dreaming Room in December 2005. The same feeling, the same rush of shame, the same deep embarrassment I had felt back then in 1975 when I drove back with Arnie to his home to talk about my epiphany, only to discover the huge wall that loomed before me between what I promised to do and what I would need to do to keep that promise to Bob.

I was standing in front of my first audience of twenty-seven Dreamers, on the weekend of December 8, 9, and 10, 2005, in a conversation with a man called Gunny, a top-flight pilot from Desert Storm, discussing a problem he was having with his business in New Orleans in the aftermath of Katrina. I was in the middle of a sentence whereby I was helping him to better understand why he was having such a difficult time dealing with the circumstances he found himself in, and a sudden flash of embarrassment washed over me like a red wave. Who in the world was I to tell this man what to do? How could I possibly believe in what I was saying? This was a man who had flown an F-16 into battle every day for months and had been shot at, had ridden out a huge natural disaster in New Orleans, had started up a new reconstruction company in the middle of all that, and was now here, asking me to help him.

I was suddenly caught in the absurdity of it all, the reaction that comes from within, which says, "Who are you to tell this man anything? Who are you to advise him? What could you possibly know that could be of any value to this man? Who do you think you are?" Understand, all of this came to me in the hot flash of a second, in between one word and the one that was to follow it. As I caught myself standing in front of these twenty-seven people looking intently at me, as I engaged with Gunny, he saw something in that exchange with me that I was deeply questioning. He saw exactly what he had come to me to see—a way out. A way to both transcend his troubling experiences in New Orleans, and to transform them.

And it had come through me even as I was doubting myself. It had come through me even as it had many years before in that car with Arnie. It had come through me as though I wasn't there at all. It had come through me to express to me what I now consider to be the immensity of awe.

# STOP
## AND
# FOCUS

## The Negative Reaction

*The challenge of the negative reaction is that it can kill your imagination. It can kill it immediately because it finds within you not only the entrepreneur who has awakened so slightly, but the dark side of the entrepreneur—the one who knows that this dream that is waking you up is a fantasy that threatens to destroy you.*

*It is literally that dangerous to your normal way of life, this imagination, this dreaming, this creative burst. It threatens to destroy you because it knows you don't know what you are getting yourself into.*

*Remember how many times you have been called to pursue an opportunity only to awaken the voice within you who began to question your reasons. "What do you really know about this?" the voice asks. "How much do you think this will cost?" the voice questions. "Remember how many times you've done this before, and failed?" the voice reminds you. "Who do you think you are?" the voice challenges, knowing that that reminder alone is often enough to kill any idea you had of going down a new and unknown path.*

*Stop now and focus. Remember all the cautionary voices in your life. Place them with the people they belong to. Ask yourself what those people have ever done that put them in what they believed to be harm's way. What happened? Why did it happen?*

*(continued)*

*What is it about you that listens so intently to the voices who caution you about taking risks? What do risks look like to you? Why are they risks? What is so risky about taking risks? And why does this always happen to you exactly when the entrepreneur begins to awaken?*

*Stop and focus. Look closely. Experience the conflict. Let go of it. Be where you are, now. Repeat that experience. Experience the conflict. Let go of it. Be where you are, now. There is only this experience, now. There is nothing more you have to do but experience it.*

# 7

# The Personal Dream

This dream is the natural state of man.
We live in this dream as we live in the air, and would
be hopeless if we were not able to realize sometimes that
we live not only in this world, but also in another world,
where it is possible for us to awaken to different
perceptions, to another way of being, of thinking and
of feeling. The act of waking up can change everything;
it is to be born to another world within oneself.

—Henri Traco, *The Taste of Things That Are True*

There are many kinds of dreams. There is the dream of the lonely man or woman, there is the dream of the lustful lover, there is the dream of the old man wishing to become young, of the young man wishing to be older, of the spinster wishing for a companion, of the companion wishing for a lover. There is the dream of the "D" student wishing for good grades, of the single mother wishing her son would get a job, of the plain woman wishing for beauty.

All of these dreams are what can be called "personal dreams." They, and so many more just like them, from the sublime to the absurd, from the realistic to the fantastic, are what consume most people most of the time. For most of us, they remain dreams of long-ing, of personal desire.

But, even when such dreams convert into action, they rarely if ever produce the desired result. They may become goals, but the goals themselves are suspect once one has achieved them. Once one is made less plain by the surgeon's knife, once one has found his or her lover, once one has built the five-thousand-square-foot house on the hill, with a swimming pool behind it, once one has created those incredi-ble abs after exercising for month after strenuously hopeful month, still, each and every one of those personal dreamers find themselves exactly the same in the end, longing for more, for better, for the inde-finable something the dream was to have provided them, but never does.

And then it goes on, a bigger house, a better tan, a faster car, a more responsive lover. All these personal dreams are found out to be, if we are lucky, not only empty, but a foolish, and therefore tragic, waste of our time. They never deliver the goods our imaginations so hopefully promised us. They never give us more life.

I call these personal dreams "incremental dreams." Incremental because when they are fulfilled we are now in need of other dreams to pursue to replace them. There is no end to them! They are the fuel that energizes our otherwise dispassionate lives. They are the promise at the end of our personal rainbow. They are not only what we dreamed about as kids—who or what we want to be when we grow up, the fame, the fortune, the hero, the adventurer—but they follow us and fuel us for the rest of our lives as adults.

Yet, even when we become the hero we dreamed about, even when we become the next Tiger Woods, it is never enough. The per-sonal dream always disappoints us. It's as though it was a prelude to life, not life itself.

The shine of it goes away, the joy of it goes away, the look of it goes quickly away. It is as if there can be no rest from the continued disappointment of the personal dream. In time, doesn't everything personal leave us longing for something else personal?

That is why the awakened entrepreneur does not awaken to the personal dream, but rather to the impersonal one.

# STOP
### AND
# FOCUS

## The Personal Dream

*How many personal dreams have you had? Write them down, as many as you can remember. What happens to them? How many cars have you bought? What happened to them? How many awards have you sought? What happened to you after you won them? How many new things have you bought? What happened to them after you bought them?*

*Stop and focus on the nature of personal dreams. What do they feel like when you first have them? When you begin to pursue them? When you either succeed at realizing them or fail to do so? What is the reality of personal dreams in your life?*

*Feel what it means to be you when you are pursuing the fulfillment of a personal dream. Feel what it means to be you when you succeed in getting what you wanted. See the continuity of your life as it goes from one personal dream to another and to yet another.*

*Stop and focus on the nature of personal dreaming. Feel it as deeply as you can.*

# 8

# The Impersonal Dream

Everything vanishes around me, and works are born as if
out of the void. Ripe, graphic fruits fall off. My hand has
become the obedient instrument of a remote will.

—Paul Klee

What do I mean when I say "the impersonal dream"? I mean
just that—it is anything but personal. It is not about you
and it is not about me. It is about the act of creativity, about that
"sudden seeing" of a possibility we have never seen before, when we
suddenly become aware, intensely aware, of some condition, some reality, some frozen particle of time and space that is just dying to be
fixed, or changed, or reinvented, or transformed.

Because of what we, as entrepreneurs, do about that which we
dream, there exists a reality that brings more happiness into the world
than was (or wasn't) there before. A woman in poverty can live without poverty. A light is turned on in a little hut where there is no
electricity. Water flows clear and clean where the water was once inadequate and filthy. Children who were starving now have food because someone found a way to produce it. A young, up-and-coming
executive learns the key skills she needs to get ahead.

On a lot less ambitious scale, a cell phone becomes a camera. A camera becomes a television. A car becomes a boat, a boat an airplane. Today, a business can be put anywhere we want it to be, because we can now do whatever we wish to do from anywhere.

It's all impersonal to the one who creates it, yet it is personal to the one who buys it. The impersonal, in this context, simply means it's not about me.

Do you get what I mean? Entrepreneurship is nothing about the one who *creates* a thing and everything about the one who *consumes* a thing. Entrepreneurs don't care about the thing they create, in and of itself (as much as they may love what they produce or do). They care about creating it because of the impact it can have on someone else. It's about that thing as an answer to a question others have long ago stopped asking, or long before they even considered the possibility of it changing for them.

The first question for the awakened entrepreneur is, "What good would this thing I am thinking of creating do for the one who buys it? And why is that important? And how long will that be important?" For after all, to the entrepreneur, the company he or she is about to create is not a disposable thing, but a thing that will, hopefully, last a long, long time.

The thing an entrepreneur is inventing is of value to the degree it has lasting value. To whom? To the customer. To the one who consumes it.

Do people consume companies? Yes, of course they do. A great company is consumable to the degree it was invented only with the customer in mind. Its stock is consumed, in that people buy it. Its products are consumed in that people buy them. Its services are consumed, to the degree that people buy them and use them and enjoy them and benefit from them.

So, a company that is created as a product of a truly impersonal dream, which is not about the entrepreneur but about the customer, is what entrepreneurs always create. No matter how much they believe in it, can't live without it, consume it themselves because they love what they invented and can't imagine anyone else not loving it, the entrepreneur knows that there is only one justifiable reason for creating a company: to serve someone else's desire better than anyone has ever done before.

Here's where that gets tricky. The awakened entrepreneur in this new age of the entrepreneur makes choices for his or her customer long before the customer does. The customer is not aware that he wants what the entrepreneur invents, not until long after the entrepreneur has invented it. In fact, you might ask customers if they want something the entrepreneur intends to invent and, for the life of them, they couldn't tell you why in the world anyone would want such a thing, or why such a business would be important, or meaningful, or desirable, at all. A fax machine wasn't invented because anyone wanted one. A television set wasn't invented because anyone wanted one. A car wasn't invented because anyone wanted one. In fact, it took a long, long time for anyone to appreciate an automobile, even though it was available for customers to buy.

The same principle applies to a refrigerator, or a dishwasher, or a hair dryer, or a lawn mower that you drive like a tractor because now you *can*. What husband ever said to his wife, "I need a tractor to mow our lawn!" She would have thought he was nuts.

What an entrepreneur creates has meaning, and that's why it creates money. It doesn't work the opposite way: Creating money does not give the created thing meaning.

But, meaning, in this new age of the entrepreneur—in this renaissance of meaning, in this new world where meaning is all the rage—this meaning means something significantly greater than just any old meaning.

The meaning of meaning in this age of the new entrepreneur means that you must reach further than simply to do something meaningful . . . make a good tire, bake a good pizza, deliver a good shoeshine, or whatever else you have gone into business to do . . . You must reach much further to a point beyond the ordinary. You must reach much, much deeper than simply creating more choices, or lower prices, or faster delivery. No, in this age of the entrepreneur, in this age of the impersonal dreamer, you must kick ass in ways no one ever thought possible.

■

At the outset, Arnie and I were not so much in disagreement; it was if we were living in different worlds. His was the world of work. Mine was the world of creating what works.

Arnie was full up with doing the work of his business, writing ads, creating advertising strategies, designing advertising, and marketing campaigns. I was full up with the question of building a process and a system through which Arnie's work would translate into sales for his clients.

The clients wanted that. As a result, the clients wanted me. Client One turned into Client Two, which quickly turned into Client Six. I now had an office in Arnie's advertising agency, working with his clients to add value to his services by getting his clients ready for the leads that would come their way once the ads did what they were supposed to do.

Arnie had never gone into the process with his clients that deeply before. It was as though Arnie had set a limit to what his company was supposed to do. There was a border Arnie never crossed in his client's business, the border called "inside the business." Arnie sent leads to the client's door and went back to the media to get more. Sometimes sales were made, and other times they weren't, but according to Arnie's philosophy that wasn't his job. It was the client's job.

That felt like a strange thing to me. How could he draw such an artificial line? If the lead was dropped at the client's door, wouldn't it be only natural for Arnie to walk in with it and say, "So, now what are we going to do with this?"

But, Arnie didn't. So I did. And that created a lot of new business for Arnie's advertising agency, but a lot of problems as well. Suddenly, Arnie's clients expected him to walk the lead into the door and follow it wherever it went from there. That was my job, but it became Arnie's job as well. After all, if a lead was not converted into a sale, it put the ad that attracted it into question. Without warning, Arnie was immersed in questions he had never really bothered or intended to ask. What kind of leads was he generating? Of what value were those leads? Did they convert easily? If so, why? If not, why?

That introduced Arnie to an unfamiliar new world—the world of the systems thinker. The world where I unwittingly found myself with Arnie at my side, and us saying to each other, "What in the world is this?" I loved it. Arnie hated it. Because it really mucked up the simple world in which he lived.

This is exactly what I confronted in the Dreaming Room. I never would have anticipated that the pursuit of the impersonal could be so challenging to so many people. "What do you want?" I would ask a Dreaming Room participant. The response would be the description of a personal dream—a picture of the dreamer in the perfect house with the perfect family living the perfect life in a perfect world where everything was beautiful, where money was never a problem.

As with Arnie, all anyone wanted in the Dreaming Room was work they loved to do so they could make the money they needed to get the things they wanted and more. To each and every Dreaming Room participant, that was what dreaming meant. And if their dream included creating, the creating it included was also all about them, as opposed to the creation. The creation in all cases was a reflection of them.

The Dreaming Room revealed to me how hopelessly narcissistic we all are. But, as I dug deeper, as we pursued the question deeper, it also became apparent to me that the people in the Dreaming Room were also longing for something bigger than they were. They were hoping for something to appear in their lives that would wake them up out of their narcissistic torpor. They were, many of them, tired of themselves! Tired of listening to themselves, looking at themselves, being with themselves, doing what they were hopelessly programmed to do every morning when they got up, and every night when they got ready for bed.

They were looking for something, even though many had stopped looking. They were wishing for something even though many had stopped wishing. They were tired. That's what it was. They were bone-weary tired. Tired of living. I would never have imagined that to be true—that all of the people who came to the Dreaming Room had all but given up. Even though their lives were chockful of doing whatever they were up to, they were resigned to never truly figuring life out, business out, themselves out. "Who am I?" was a question they had all long ago stopped asking in favor of "What's next?"

# STOP

### AND

# FOCUS

## *The Impersonal Dream*

*This is more difficult than you could ever imagine: trying to come to the place where you don't matter, and only the customer matters.*

*Stop and focus on that for a moment. See the customer. See him. See her. The only thing that matters to the entrepreneur is what his or her customer wants. The entrepreneur wants to treat his or her customer better than anyone else.*

*It goes out, not in? That's exactly where the entrepreneurial focus must go. Out, not in. Do you see why the invention of a business of your own has nothing to do with what you want? Unless, of course, what you want has only to do with your customer, not with you? That the impersonal dream lives in someone else, and not in you? That the sudden seeing of that, the amazing clarity about that, the excitement that comes from that is where the true entrepreneurial action is?*

*Stop now and focus on an impersonal dream. Name one. Then two. Then three. Go for as long as you can, focusing on a customer who needs something he or she can't get, who wants something no*

*(continued)*

*one yet has provided to him or her. You are right now beginning the true work of the entrepreneur. And to do that work truly, you must stop and focus for as long and as deep as you possibly can. Yes, this is where the action is. This is the beginning of a dream that has meaning.*

# 9

## The Sudden Shock

When a man journeys into a far country, he must be
prepared to forget many of the things he has learned, and
to acquire such customs that are inherent with existence
in the new land; he must abandon the old ideals and the
old gods, and oftentimes he must reverse the very codes
by which his conduct has hitherto been shaped.

—Jack London, "In a Far Country"

I t happens to every one of us at one or more times in our life. If
we're lucky, that is. What happens is a sudden shock. It is an absolutely necessary component of the awakening of the entrepreneur
within us. No sudden shock, no dream worth pursuing. My sudden
shock in 1975 was to see the world and each and every business
within it as a complete, unified, intelligent system.

I saw that at once. It was not something that happened over time,
even though elements of it came to me over time. It struck me all at
once. First it wasn't there, then, suddenly, it was.

This sudden shock that showed me how the world really was. And
it happened in such an unpredictable way. I had been working with
Arnie's clients, along with many new clients I began to create for
Arnie with my new and compelling story that I made up for Arnie.

Finally, an ad agency that not only creates leads for your business, but shows you how to close them!

Wow, an ad agency that had suddenly morphed into a sales agency! We don't create ads, we create sales.

Business began to boom for Arnie. And of course, if it boomed for Arnie, it would boom for me. Because I was the one on the firing line, I was the one who had to deliver on Arnie's ad agency's promise. I was the one who not only sold the new business Arnie was getting, but had to deliver the promise to them.

And I did, in the form of a selling system that proved to transform Arnie's business as well as his clients' businesses. But, still something was missing. It dogged my heels everywhere I went.

Every small business I walked into seemed to be a collection of broken pieces, and seemed to fail in the most fundamental ways. If the product worked, the people didn't. If the people worked, they worked far too hard for what they earned in return. When the money went up, the pleasure seemed to go down. People argued a lot, felt little satisfaction at what they did. The places were high-tech but were low energy. All the work seemed to spiral into many unpredictable fits and starts, and nobody seemed to have a handle on it. Nobody seemed to be able to explain the whole of it, only their part of it, if that.

Understand, to me in this world of engineers, life was amazing. I couldn't understand how anybody could get bored in such a highly charged environment. Everything in Silicon Valley was new. Miracles were being created everywhere you looked, but nobody seemed to appreciate it. To me it was a candy store of opportunity; to everyone else it seemed to be business as usual.

That wasn't completely true, of course. There was a lot of excitement at Apple Computer. However, when I asked questions of managers at Apple about how their dealers' businesses worked, nobody knew anything. "It's *their* business, it's not *our* business," the Apple guys said. And when I asked the same questions of an Apple dealer, he or she would look at me like I was a lunatic. "What do you mean?"

That's how it was throughout Silicon Valley in those days as I wandered from business to small business in 1975 and 1976 working my newborn sales systems logic.

And then, in McDonald's, I suddenly saw it. Please accept my apology if you've read this before, dear reader, because I have said it in every single one of my books, that if McDonald's was not *my* Holy Grail it certainly was Ray Kroc's. And if I fail to tell you this McDonald's mythos now, you will miss the entire point of the sudden shock that awakens.

It was as if I were born again. I walked into McDonald's on a bright day, and I suddenly saw what was missing in every single business I had been counseling.

**I saw the System.**

I saw the color of it, the shape of it, the size of it, the form of it, the amazing eloquence of it, the people of it, and the rhythm of it, the sound of it, the bright, white light of it, and the bustle and extreme hustle of it, so help me God.

In this sudden moment I felt McDonald's as though it was some grand and glorious marching band! Did you ever see anything in garish, brash, primary colors look so grateful to be alive? Did you ever see kids whooping and hollering when they were simply working for the short change and the few measly dollars? Did you ever imagine you could create a happening in a hamburger stand, where kids impatiently but thankfully stood in line to get their burgers and fries or Big Macs and their tiny, tiny toys, all in a kid's box with gizmos and gadgets and puzzles and promises written all over it? Did you ever imagine something so prosaic as a hamburger and fries and a Coke could make such a ruckus? Of course not, nor could anyone else. But

Ray Kroc did, and was blessed for having done it by countless millions of moms ... no ... billions!

That's what I walked into on that day whose date I fail to remember, but I will never forget the picture it created in my mind's eye. "Wow," I thought. "I can do that!"

Anyone can! If they see it, if they feel it, if they understand the magic of it, anyone can!

And with that thought in mind, I rushed off to my next client's business to knock his unwary head off his shoulders with a story to beat the band.

# STOP
### AND
# FOCUS

## The Sudden Shock

What lessons are important to awakening the entrepreneur within you? And did my story about McDonald's have anything to do with all this? What impact did it have on my sudden seeing? What was the Shock that I spoke about?

Stop and focus. What does the Shock have to do with your life? With your potential? With your dream?

Stop and focus. Make a list as quickly as you can of the Shocks you have had in your life that enabled you to see a truth you had never seen before. What happened in each and every case? List the outcomes.

Then stop and focus on each. Do not do anything, just allow the experiences to do what they do.

Stop and focus and let your imagination do the rest.

■

# 10

## The Dream Is Born

For this is what we do. Put one foot forward and
then the other. Lift our eyes to the snarl and smile of
the world once more. Think. Act. Feel. Add our little
consequence to the tides of good and evil that flood and
drain the world. Drag our shadowed crosses into the hope
of another night. Push our brave hearts into the promise
of a new day. With love: the passionate search for a truth
other than our own. With longing: the pure ineffable
yearning to be saved. For so long as fate keeps waiting,
we live on. God help us. God forgive us. We live on.

—Gregory David Roberts, *Shantaram*

I walked out of my mother's home with the knowledge that it was
time to create something new in my life, and then I went home
and did it.

I created the Dreaming Room.

I have not looked back since.

The Dreaming Room was to be the place where people like you
and me could awaken the entrepreneur within, to give us something
to do, to commit ourselves to something that has meaning, something that moves us, that inspires us, that awakens our passion, that
calls out to us in a way very few people have ever experienced.

That is the extremely personal reward that the impersonal dream gives us.

Inevitably, people ask me, "Why impersonal? What is so important about a dream being impersonal? I have never had an impersonal dream, Michael. When I dream it's always about me."

"Yes, I understand," I reply, "but, if that's true, then you have never experienced the truly personal thrill at having created an impersonal result.

"Like when you give a complete stranger a gift they never expected.

"Like when you give your child a thrill he or she never expected.

"Like when you go to the trouble of solving a problem for someone else, really working hard to figure it out, and then solving it. And watching his or her face when you do.

"And I know you have experienced that truly personal thrill, and I know that you know there is no feeling quite like it!"

That is what the impersonal dream is.

And there is nothing more personal than when you have it! My first true entrepreneurial dream was the one I awakened to in fall 1975. It was the beginning of my next thirty years, and is still going strong. It was when I came to the realization that I was going to create a small business revolution. It was when I said to Thomas, the man who was going to be my partner for the next eight years, the man with whom I started my new venture, and without whom I would have never accomplished it, "I'm going to build a company that has the potential of transforming small business worldwide." I told Thomas, "I intend to build the McDonald's of small business consulting. I intend to transform the lives of every small business owner we can, by building a turnkey consulting system that business novices can use at a cost to our clients that is roughly the same as that of a minimum-wage employee. Just think what would happen if we could do that!"

Tom looked at me and said, "Well, what are we waiting for?"

▪

Our Dream was to transform small business worldwide.

Our Vision was to build the McDonald's of small business consulting.

Our Purpose was to transform the lives of every small business owner in the world.

Our Mission was to build the world's first turnkey consulting system so we could hire novices, turn them into experts, and deliver our services to the smallest of small businesses at no more than the cost of a minimum-wage employee so that every small business owner could afford it.

And that's exactly what we did!

Thirty-one years later, I had my second Dream, called the Dreaming Room, to inspire people to dream by awakening the entrepreneur within them.

My Vision was to create the McDonald's of new business creation.

My Purpose was to transform the lives of ordinary people by providing them with the thrill of creation while creating the means to generate their own and others' economic freedom.

My Mission was to create a turnkey system for awakening the entrepreneur within every person who wished to go into business for themselves, while providing them with the support for doing it.

And I am doing it!

▪

The Dream is what creates a new business. If it's a great dream, a great idea, it is about a great business. If it's a small dream, a small idea, it's about an ordinary business. A small dream, a small idea, creates a small business that will always be small. Only a great Dream has the power within it to create a great business. The great Dream may not actually be sufficient to create a great business, but without a great Dream there is no chance you will ever create a great business. A great business doesn't have to be a big business, but it will have the power to become one.

Without a great Dream, no business is sustainable. There's not enough energy to sustain it.

The great Dream, the entrepreneurial Dream, the intentional Dream only comes to you when you are thinking of something other than yourself, since the entrepreneurial Dream is always about someone else.

The entrepreneurial Dreamer rarely thinks in terms of what he or she wants.

The entrepreneurial Dreamer always dreams about results, as opposed to process.

The entrepreneurial Dreamer always lives in the future, imagines a result happening in the future, and when he or she sees this imagined result in the future, a problem that lives in the present is solved.

Let me say it again: The entrepreneurial Dreamer dreams about results, always results, and nothing other than results. The results are for someone else, not for the entrepreneur.

It is results that transform the world. And it is a Great Dream that creates results.

■

When I turned to Arnie and told him what I was going to do, he wasn't happy with me.

"You'll never do it," he said.

"Why not?" I asked.

"Because it's impossible," he responded. "All businesses and industries are different. All markets are different. All people and problems are different. You'll never do it."

"But, Arnie," I responded, "what if I can? What if all businesses are actually the same? What if your belief about businesses and markets and people and problems is wrong? What if there are universally applicable rules that, once discovered, would enable us to solve all of the problems all businesses face? What if that were true, then what?"

Arnie simply looked at me with disappointment all over his face. It bordered on disgust. It was as though I had just let him down in the most fundamental of ways, as though I had just become someone other than his friend.

There was nothing left for me to do but leave.

I never saw Arnie again.

# STOP
## AND
# FOCUS

# *The Dream Is Born*

*It is time to dream. It is time to care about something bigger than you. It is time to imagine something sorely needed in the world—the world you live in—that somebody would pay to have. It is time to look around you and ask yourself, "What's missing in this picture?"*

*Every place you look, if you look carefully and with interest, you will find something missing in this picture. Services aren't being provided as promised. Products aren't being delivered as promised. Nothing is easy; everything is difficult. Everywhere you look, people are doing without. Not without what there is plenty of, but without what is unavailable to them.*

*If the lawn isn't cut the way the customer wants it, something is left out. If the pool isn't serviced the way the customer wants it, something is left out. If the car isn't repaired the way the customer wants it, something is left out. The plane the customer flies on is uncomfortable. The baggage the customer is waiting for is either lost or late. The taxi the customer hails is dirty, the driver is rude, and the trip is uncomfortable and too expensive.*

*Something is always left out. What do you see around you? What's missing in the picture of your life? How many opportunities do you see waiting for you to transform into opportunities for some customer? How many ways do you see to begin the pursuit of the impossible?*

■

# PART THREE

# THE THINKER
## AND
## THE VISION

# 11

# Taking the Dream Apart

always the beautiful answer
who asks a more beautiful question.

—e.e. cummings, *Complete Poems*

When the Dreamer is done, the Thinker comes onstage. Where the Dreamer is all about What, the Thinker is all about How. The Dreamer, of course, is never really done, but there is that exquisite moment when every Dreamer knows it's time to hand off the Dream to the Thinker, without whose active engagement the Dream will float adrift.

The Dream at this stage is best described as a grand idea for a ship, but only that. The Thinker is the one who does what's needed to get it ready to sail. The Thinker knows the mathematics of shipbuilding, the logistics of ship development, the management of ship handling, the sum total of what the ship's architect, the Dreamer, intended this ship to do. And, even if the Thinker didn't know all those things, he or she would have to figure them out. Because that's what Thinkers do; they figure things out. They look at the puzzle, the picture it is intended to make, and figure out how those pieces need to come together.

The Thinker turns the Great Idea into a Great Reality.

Let's follow the process together as I lived it so many years ago.

■

Tom was my Thinker and had an amazing ability to turn every dream I had into reality. In turn, I had the same amazing ability to turn every one of Tom's dreams into reality. Not that he would have done it without me; he wouldn't. My Dream was an impersonal Dream. Tom's dreams were very, very personal. Tom wasn't truly interested in transforming small business worldwide. He was interested in getting what he wanted when we transformed business worldwide . . . the fame, the fortune, the lifestyle we would have if we could pull off my Dream of E-Myth, if we could turn it into reality. Tom quickly became consumed by it.

As we got started, Tom's massive intelligent energy was of the constructive kind. He said, "Oh, that's what you want," and would immediately begin to design it. He would design practically, what I conceived of abstractly. He would simply begin to build, sentence by sentence, paragraph by paragraph, a rough model of what he thought I meant.

We would do that creating and building at the outset, months before we ever opened our doors, nonstop, every day. I started of course with a question. The question was "How do we build a business development program that has the power to transform small business worldwide?"

A second question followed directly on the heels of the first. This question was "What does a small business owner need that he or she doesn't have?"

Immediately following those two questions began the answers. Actually suppositions, at first. Always suppositions. I believe, now, looking back on the entire thirty-year process, that we are still operating at E-Myth Worldwide under suppositions that have not truly resolved themselves into anything other than the continuous, unending process of searching for the answer to those questions, and arriving at new and better—and sometimes, worse—suppositions in an attempt to come to the final answer to those first two questions. And here I am today, writing this book, still hotly engaged in those questions as I pursue them with you.

We quickly came to some answers back in 1977 that would serve as the foundation for everything we did over the next few years. The answers we came to, however, were not only a product of the Thinker, but the experience Tom and I had with the clients I developed walking down the street learning how to sell our services, door to door, cold-calling on small businesses in San Mateo, California, where our first offices were.

The first and most fundamental answers Tom and I came to were these:

■ **All businesses require a Vision.** To develop a Vision called for a process. Our first job, then, was to build the Visioning Process that we would then deliver to our clients to help them formulate a Vision of their own. A business without a Vision has no soul; a business without a soul has no heart, no passion. A business without passion is a business whose demise has already been foretold.

■ **All Visions are both personal and impersonal.** A Vision is comprised of your primary aim and your strategic objective. The first is the Vision for your life. The second is the Vision for your business. Together, these two Visions combined to make one Vision that would become the driving force for the growth of the company. Tom and I built these two processes and used them at the very beginning to direct our clients forward toward the development of their business. These two processes asked the question, "What do you want?" That became the linchpin for everything that was to follow in the Michael Thomas Business Development Program, which became the E-Myth Mastery Program, the system that stands at the heart of everything we do with our clients today at E-Myth Worldwide.

Interestingly, when we first told our clients what we needed to do to turn their business around, they balked at the idea. They thought it highly impractical. Every one of our clients believed that all they really needed was more sales and/or better people. We persisted, however, knowing that without a clear idea of where they were headed our clients didn't stand a chance of getting there.

■ **Every company is an organization,** an organization of work, and, subsequently, an organization of people. That calls for the development of an organization chart. The organization chart was essential no matter how small the business was. The organization chart described quite eloquently the way the business was to work, where the accountability and authority rested, what the relationships between functions were and how they were exercised, which functions were primary, which secondary, which tertiary. The organization chart would flow into a flowchart demonstrating the way work would flow in the company as it went about its business of fulfilling its strategic objective. Without an organization chart, Tom and I surmised, there would be no possibility of the company behaving in an organized manner. And, if the company failed to behave in an organized manner, there would be no possibility of our business development program "transforming small business worldwide" as our Dream intended our company to do.

■ **An organization is an organization of systems.** Within the organization chart there were actions for each and every component of the chart, for each component of every function, the how-we-do-this and how-we-do-that mechanics of the business. These, Tom and I called "Systems." Tom and I made the assumption in those very early days that if we were going to transform small business worldwide, we would need to identify, and then build, the universal systems that every business needed to fulfill its strategic objective. We determined that a business was nothing more or less than the sum total of the operating systems, which enabled it to keep its promise to its customers in the way it intended to do. While those systems existed in every company (therefore their universality), every company was organized in its own unique way using specialized forms of universal systems to produce its own unique result in its own unique way. In that way, Tom and I surmised, while each and every business aimed for uniqueness, it was in fact attaining that uniqueness by the way it tailored universal systems to act in a proprietary manner. Therefore, we concluded that one of our company's unique deliverables needed to be a method for inspiring, training, and coaching our clients on the identification of the systems in their organization; the way a system was shaped to deliver a uniquely branded result; the way a system was improved continuously to deliver a better result in concert with all the other systems in their company; and what we called the "Systems Imperative": All systems merge into one system and that one system is the company's core operating system, which every manager within the company must come to understand, respect, and support completely. Thus, Tom and I began to use every chance we could get to express our mantra, "The System is the Solution." "You've gotta become a Systems Thinker" also became an expression we used frequently with our own people, our clients, and our prospective clients.

■

We had set out with a Dream, and were now building it brick by brick. We were conceptualizing how the world worked in our own limited but passionate fashion, simply because we needed to if we were going to actually do what we had set out to do: to transform small business worldwide. And, as we did this thing, we built the structure of the Dream so that we could actually begin to see it, so that we could actually begin to *do* it.

■

It's important for you to realize something about the four fundamental answers listed above—call them Tom's and my "agreements." Prior to their arising and becoming the fundamentals they came to represent in all our conversations with ourselves, our new employees, and our many, many new clients, we came also to many not so obvious and very distracting conclusions. We spent an entire year and a half at the very beginning of our company's development writing standardized action plans as solutions to our clients' confusion about planning.

These action plans offered obvious step-by-step clarity. "This is how you design a brochure." "This is how you create an organization chart." "This is how you create an order entry system." And on and on and on. There were dozens of them and no end in sight.

Instead of turning our clients on, they turned our clients very much off. Why, we had no idea. But, over that time, we began to better understand it. While our clients wanted order, they were unwilling (call it insufficiently disciplined) to follow the steps we laid out for them. While we could describe quite precisely how to do it, nobody would follow the instructions unless we mandated them to do it. And we were in no position to mandate our clients to do anything of the kind. So, we ultimately were forced to abandon it.

That wasn't the first and not the last of the false paths Tom and I took together to figure out the secret. Thousands upon thousands of hours were spent applying the dedication and the inspiration and the application of the Thinker in the invention of "the McDonald's of small business consulting" as we called it. And yet, with all that, our Vision was slow to develop. We had an inkling of what we wanted, but we couldn't for the life of us give you an engineer's description of it. Not yet, we couldn't.

# STOP
## AND
# FOCUS

## *Taking the Dream Apart*

*This relationship between your Dreamer and your Thinker is a very delicate one. Don't forget that the Dreamer and Thinker can be two separate people, or they can be two facets of one entrepreneur. If the Dreamer becomes overwhelmed by the Thinker's incredible left-brain energy (as can easily happen . . . after all, what is a dream but a vaporous idea that has never been real before?), the whole enterprise can quickly come tumbling down.*

*To prevent that, you must take your Dream apart, study every minute detail, and then put it back together again to see what it looks like. So when your Dreamer begins to doubt his or her judgment, ask this question: "What do I want?" Ask it as frequently as you can. And then answer it by a restatement of your Dream as articulately as you can. Your Dream is more important at this point than your Vision. More important than anything else. Your Dream is everything. It will form the justification for your enterprise. You need to develop as many different ways to express it as possible. You need to find reasons in the world that say, "So this is why you're so passionate about your Dream! Aha, I get it!" You need to solicit feedback by sharing your Dream with as many people as possible, asking them to support your cause by sending you stories and facts that will help you achieve it.*

*You also need to pay attention to your Dream every day. Tell stories about your Dream every day. Especially now when you've invited your Thinker to help you left-brain it. The Thinker is the left-brained side of the right-brained Dreamer who, as a now intelligently emerging and evolving creator, is beginning the rich, incredibly creative process of inventing your new enterprise: what it does, how it does it, why it does it that way, and how it makes money. You, as the awakening new entrepreneur, are not only here to embrace your Dream, but to protect and defend it. All it* has *is you. Because all it* is *is you.*

# 12

# Taking the Dream Apart Again

Mysteries are irresistible to me, and a trail is
something that *must* be followed until it gives up
its secret or puts me onto the trail of something
even more amazing. Tracks fascinate me.

—*The Tracker: The True Story of Tom Brown, Jr.*

In the Dreaming Room, I came to the realization that my Dream
of awakening the Entrepreneur within my fellow participants was
something quite different from what I thought it would be. I was
faced with the challenge of trusting my judgment and intuition with
an entire array of people that I had never met. I knew nothing whatsoever about them, what was working and what wasn't in their lives
and in their businesses, what business they were in, or what business
they wished to be in, and what their single biggest problem was. All I
knew was that I had promised to turn their single biggest problem
into their single biggest opportunity.

What they didn't know, and what I was beginning to, was that to
pull off this miraculous feat I would need to call upon my Dreamer,
Thinker, Storyteller, and Leader, sometimes one more than another,
sometimes another more than the other one. I had no idea whatso-

ever what that would look like before doing it on behalf of each and every person in the room—thirty-five people on average—and all in no more than two and a half days.

When I opened my first Dreaming Room on December 8, 2005, I had absolutely no experience at doing what I was proposing to do . . . absolutely none. Oh, I had spoken to many, many audiences of five to ten thousand people. But never had I engaged so personally, so intimately, so aggressively with any one audience like I was going to be called upon to do in that very first weekend Dreaming Room.

The Dreamer had a dream all right, but until I walked into that room I had yet to have a conversation with my Thinker. I had to come face-to-face with whatever was going to show up, all alone and on my own best behavior.

I have no idea to this day how I pulled it off, but I did. I simply let go. When I am moved by a Dream, when my vision is being created, my purpose comes alive and the mission simply takes over. And when that happens I have learned to get out of the way and simply allow it to happen.

What also happens in those extraordinary moments that last the entire weekend, is that the Dreamer in me wakes up and can see in full relief everything that is taking place—all movement, all insights, all impact—as though frozen in time.

My Thinker, my left-brained ally, while this is all going on, is conceiving the processes, systems, and scalability factor in everything that I am doing, so that we can systematize it to use again with another person, and then another, and then yet another. . . .

# STOP
## AND
# FOCUS

## *Taking the Dream Apart Again*

*If your Vision were to faithfully replicate McDonald's, how would you go about it? Where would you start? How would you even think about it?*

*Say your Dream was to transform the way medical services are provided to senior citizens. Start thinking about it. Do you start by doing research on medical services for senior citizens? Or do you start thinking about what it feels like to be a senior citizen? And what kind of senior citizen are we talking about? A senior citizen with few financial problems, who is well insured, or a senior citizen who is not insured and has little discretionary income? Are we speaking about a senior citizen who lives with his or her family or a senior citizen who is living on his or her own? Are we thinking about a senior citizen who is living in a rest home or an assisted care center? Are we talking about a senior citizen who is active or a senior citizen who has stopped participating in their community?*

*There are a host of questions we need to ask as we begin the process of converting our Dream into a moving and intelligent Vision. And that it is here where we are attempting to bring our Dream down to earth where we can see it, touch it, feel it, and do it.*

*Wouldn't you want to begin to talk to a lot of senior citizens*

*(continued)*

*who fit the model of the senior citizens who will benefit from your Dream of transforming the medical services they receive? What does it feel like to be them as they make an appointment with their medical care provider? What's going on in their minds? What does it feel like to be waiting for the doctor's conclusions? What does it feel like to be them following their visit, going home, being who they are, elderly people approaching the end of their lives? What questions, fears, and thoughts do they have on their minds?*

■

# 13

## The Vision Begins to Take Form

The painter has to wrestle with color, canvas and brushes,
the sculptor with stone and chisel . . . yet, the creative act,
their "vision" of what they are going to create,
transcends time. It is the same for every manifestation
of being. The experience of loving, of joy, of grasping
truth does not occur in time, but in the here and now.
*The here and now is eternity . . .*

—Erich Fromm, *To Have or to Be*

As Tom and I dug deeper into our Vision, as we began to get a taste of what our system would look like if it were to be able to transform small business worldwide, we began to see it more literally, rather than figuratively, as had been the case up to this point.

We began to imagine hiring kids at minimum wage, just like the kids who work at McDonald's. We began to imagine creating a system through which these kids would inspire our clients, train our clients, coach our clients, the dress code they'd follow, the tools they'd use so that our "French fries" didn't fall on the floor.

We began to imagine the colors we would use on the walls, on the sign, on the logo, on our stationery, on the client binders, on the floors and ceilings, on the tables and chairs, just as McDonald's did.

Not like any office anyone had ever seen. Not like a consulting company, but like a fast-food company, because that's exactly what we imagined we were building—the fast food of small business consulting.

We weren't selling consulting, we were selling extremely low-cost predictability like no service any small business owner had ever bought. We had artist's renderings done of our imagined kids in their uniforms, in the imagined store, with the golden arches shining overhead.

"What are our golden arches going to look like?" Tom and I continued to ask. "Draw me one," I told our artist. And he did. But it didn't look right, so he drew it again. And then again. We went on like that, testing one look and then another, and then yet another. The company was beginning to take shape in our heads.

During that time, I would knock on doors in the search for the clients who would fuel our business development program and would contribute to our process of inventing our company, until Tom and I were no longer needed on the front end of the business, selling it and delivering it. Instead, we could replace ourselves with our first kids: one to sell what we did using the client acquisition system I was creating, the other to deliver it with the client fulfillment system Tom and I were creating. We knew that without that, our company could never become what we envisioned.

Tom and I could see it—the largest company of our kind in the world. It was that Vision that possessed us. It was that Vision that electrified us. It was that Vision that we continued to describe to each and every one of our new clients with such great passion that they began to believe us, and even began to do the very same thing themselves: create a Vision they could talk about to their business associates and friends.

"These two crazy guys in San Mateo are doing something nobody has ever done before," they would say to their business associates and friends. "You've got to hear them talk about it!"

People would come to hear me tell our story, and they would walk away half believing in it. And I would tell it again and again and again and more and more people began to believe it, and they would send their friends. The company became a reality built on little more than Tom's and my shared imagination.

"Can you see it?" I would ask our growing audience of business owners. And they would answer, "Yes!" "Can you see it?" I would ask again. And they would respond with even more conviction, "Yes!"

The system we were creating became much more over time than simply a system of ideas. It had become a system of action. It had become an intelligent process through which every essential thing that needed to happen in a business to enable it to grow would be done. And all of the components of those overarching systems would integrate with all of the other overarching systems to form one overarching operating system that would mirror, as it took form, the system that McDonald's had become. Much later, Starbucks, Wal-Mart, and so many other franchiselike companies followed suit and began operating with intensity because the creators of those companies were systems thinkers, just as we intended our clients to become.

Meanwhile, Tom's and my original "four agreements" turned into six, then eight, then ten. They stood for what we were now calling "The Ten Pillars of the Most Successful Small Business in the World." We imagined that Ray Kroc would agree with us, that, yes, we had identified the Ten Pillars underlying the continued success of Mc-Donald's, indeed, underlying the continued success of any great company. These Ten Pillars were, and still are, the following. (I am going to repeat the first four agreements in abbreviated form, because they truly bear repeating.)

- **All businesses require a Vision.**
- **All Visions are both personal and impersonal.**
- **Every company is an organization.**
- **An organization is an organization of systems.**

If you need to review the first four agreements in more detail, refer back to page 75. If you're still with me, here are the remaining six of the "Ten Pillars."

- **There is no such thing as customer service.** There is only customer commitment, which comes down to making an outrageous promise to your customer that you keep every single time. That outrageous promise becomes your brand. Your brand is built on your word, and it is reflected in every decision you make and every action you take. Everyone in your business must understand and be an expert at the part they are to play in keeping your promise to your customer. The effectiveness of every system in your business must be validated based on the function it plays in keeping your business's promise to your customer, and how well it keeps it. If not, then what are you going to do about it?

- **Master the money** from the bottom of the business to the top of the business. Everyone in your business must become a Master of Money. Without that there is no understanding of the truth of your business. The truth of the business resides in the truth of the money. What money does your business make, and how does it make it, and how efficiently does it make it? These are critical questions, which will drive the truth of your business into every conversation you have with your people.

■ **Your people are not your business,** and conversely, your business is not your people, either. Your business is its own reality, which includes your people, but which is not your people. Your people are themselves interested in themselves; they are only interested in your business to the degree it provides them with what they want for themselves. That is how it should be, which means that your business must possess a philosophy that provides your people with what they want, provided they give your business what it needs—and that is to keep your business's promise to your customers every single time. There are standards that come into play in this method, and you must know what those standards are, which, once agreed upon, become the rules of the game in your business. Every great business possesses rules of the game. No rules of the game, no business.

■ **Your business is an idea.** It is either a great idea or a bad idea. There are no other ideas worth talking about. If it's a great idea it's worth doing. If it's a bad idea, get out as quickly as you can.

■ **You know more about your business than anyone else does.** You can't hire people who know as much about your business as well as you do. If you can, you are in the wrong business. You need to inspire, educate, train, and coach your people to know what you know about your business, so they eventually know as much about your business as you do. Only then can your people improve your business. Until then, all they can do is harm your business.

■ **A business must mean something** if it's to be able to make a difference in the world it serves. For it to mean something it has to do something that means something. The meaning of your business is directly tied to the results it produces. If it produces meaningful results for its customer and its employees, that's what it means. "What do the results your business produces mean?" is the only meaningful question you can ask about your business.

The Michael Thomas Corporation (later E-Myth Worldwide) was definitely becoming something Tom and I could identify as The Michael Thomas Corporation. And, as the local business community got to know us better, they could, too. What MTC did and the way it did it was easily the only place in the world where a small business owner could buy what we did. And what we did and the way that we did it made an enormously positive impact on both our clients' lives and their businesses. We were well on the path to turning our Dream into our Vision.

Thank you, Tom, for what you brought to our shared Vision.

# STOP
### AND
# FOCUS

## *The Vision Begins to Take Form*

*As you can tell, when you move from the Dream Stage to the Vision Stage of your company, the form of your company becomes specific as opposed to general, and the specificity is likely to beg you to ask more questions than you're capable of answering. Ask those questions! Never stop asking those questions.*

*The answers will often shock you, or dismay you, because you have no idea how you are going to do what your answers tell you to do. What is your McDonald's? What is your business an unlikely version of? Who is your success model? Why is it your success model? What are the characteristics of your success model that make it your success model? What company are you emulating? What are you saying to the world about your new idea for a company that works better than any other . . . so that you are impassioned by it, and when you speak about it, it becomes clear to the people you are speaking to that yes, of course, that is surely incredible, there is no doubt about it, if you could do that, why, of course it would be great.*

*But of course you really can't do that. Can you? A medical service that works as well as a Grand Prix racing crew does? A health spa that provides stopwatch service while throwing the clock away?*

*(continued)*

*Watch for examples of unlikely excellence. Look for these examples all the time. In magazines, in the news, on the street.*

*Think kick-ass quality. Put that in your brain. Think about what the words* kick-ass quality *mean . . . in every aspect of your business . . . visually, emotionally, functionally, financially. Make a list of all the attributes your new company will possess. Keep a pad by your side everywhere you go and take copious notes under the categories Visual, Emotional, Functional, Financial. Remember, creating a Vision is as much about Dreaming as creating a Dream is.*

*You can never take too many notes. Write notes wherever you are. Get a memo pad and call it "Notes to Myself." As you continue reading this book, write "Notes to Myself" reflecting on the insights you are accumulating as you read. Insights, insights, insights. This book is all about insight, impressions, uncommon impressions, unlikely insights. This is not a do-it-yourself manual. It is an entrepreneurial spiritual guidebook. We are climbing the mountain together. As you are reading this book, you are also dreaming about your new business, visualizing it, imagining it, creating it. You are doing the work of an entrepreneur at this very moment! Remember that.*

# 14

# The Vision Continues
# to Take Form

We are stronger than we know. Like deep wells,
we have a capacity for sustained creative action.
Our lost dreams can come home to us.

—Julia Cameron, *Finding Water: The Art of Perseverance*

Yes, the Vision does continue to take form. Without a clearly defined Vision, the Dream is aborted. Your Dreamer unconsciously
knows this (and consciously as well, but will rarely admit to it), but
resists the work of it nonetheless. The Thinker needs to be patient
with the Dreamer at this point in the process. He or she needs to learn
how to nurse the Dreamer along.

■

Tom and I persisted, as we were fashioning The Michael Thomas Corporation, both in our minds and in our actions. Every day we came
together with a new unforeseen question: "Why are we doing it this
way? What would we do instead?" You might ask "how?" as opposed

to "what?" But, in order to know *how*, we needed to first be entirely confident about *what*.

It shocked us how easily we forgot the Dream, so we painted the mantra on our company walls: "Bringing the Dream Back to American Business" in bright red, white, and blue.

Why "American business" and not "business worldwide"? Because, we reasoned, if we could bring the Dream back to American business, we could bring the Dream back to any business anywhere in the world.

Why not American *small* business? Because we reasoned that since small business accounted for the vast majority of business in America (and the world), if we brought the Dream back to American small business we would bring the Dream back to all American business, and so we simply stated the conclusion as we saw it: by transforming small business we were transforming all business, and since transforming all business was bigger than transforming small business, we simply left out the word "small."

Besides, saying "American business" gave us the sense of size we were determined the company would eventually have. We were head over heels in love with the idea. "Bringing the Dream Back to American Business," yeah, you bet we would. We were actually doing it every day; it wasn't a promise for the future, it was a fact right now. Every time we sat down with a small business client, we were bringing the Dream back to American business, "one small business owner at a time!" So, we added it to our slogan on the wall. And as we did, Tom and I smiled at each other. And our clients smiled as well.

■

As Tom and I worked dutifully and inspirationally with each and every one of our clients, we also worked on the deliverables we created, along with the processes we used to deliver them. The deliverables themselves became known as Business Development Processes. They quickly demonstrated the obvious—that while we were consulting with our clients, we were quickly moving from a consulting mode to a coaching mode and, in order to coach our clients, the processes we were developing became our coaching tools.

And as we realized that, we also saw the need for warehousing our processes in a Business Development Library of Processes, which, in turn, called for an organizational hierarchy for that library, a number system within the key categories in which each process became resident content, from A to Z.

The key categories became what we now call the Seven Centers of Management Attention. We identified them as Leadership, Marketing, Money, Management, Client Fulfillment, Lead Generation, and Lead Conversion. All that was needed then was to begin the process of identifying all the material to be included in our Business Development Library of Processes within the seven categories we identified as essential for any business to be successfully grown.

The key to the library's success, however, was not its content—although, of course, content is critical—but its context. The form it took was driven by the requirements of an entrepreneurial-driven company. The library began to form itself into the three stages of a small business owner's transformation. Stage One: Getting Your House in Order; Stage Two: Growing Your Business; Stage Three: Getting Free of Your Business. You'll note that I said the three stages mirrored the small business *owner's* transformation, as opposed to the small *business's* transformation. That was because the entire process of business development was truly dependent upon our realization that, while we were working on the owner's business, we were really working on the owner himself or herself; unless or until the owner changed his or her perspective about business, the business itself would never improve. It was the owner who needed to "get his house in order." It was the owner who needed to "grow," and it was the owner who needed to "get free of the business."

Thus, the structure of our business development program, while ostensibly all about business, was really to become the most amazingly comprehensive personal development program ever devised. Its purpose was to transform an owner of a business into a chief executive officer of his or her business, and, eventually, into a stunningly effective entrepreneur in any business he or she chose to create.

As soon as that became clear to us, and as soon as we had created the hierarchy for the organization of our "library," it also became clear that for the library to be functional, each and every process needed to connect to each and every other process, much like *Great Books of the Western World*, Mortimer Adler's wonderful encyclopedia of the Western world's great thinkers and great thoughts, all tied together with his ingenious Syntopicon, the index to the great thoughts in the great books so the reader could pursue a subject, like love, and discover what every one of the great thinkers had thought about it.

That's what Tom and I aspired to do (but have not yet done)—to create a *Great Works of the Business World*, with a Syntopicon as an index to everything one would need to know about every subject dealing with the creation and operation and growth of a business. Nonetheless, we did accomplish a significant part of it by linking all of the processes in our library to one another, mirroring the point of view that served as the foundation for the entire library, which we later called the E-Myth Point of View. (For more about that, please read *The E-Myth Revisited, The E-Myth Manager,* and *E-Myth Mastery*). Thus Finance connects with Marketing connects with Management, and so on and so forth.

In short, our business development program library became the fundamental business development system that any small business owner could use to build his or her business into a consistently productive enterprise, while at the same time learning everything he or she needed to learn in order to lead that enterprise successfully.

But, we weren't quite done yet. We still needed to design the business model that would make it possible for our business to grow.

# STOP
## AND
# FOCUS

## The Vision Continues to Take Form

*What form is your business beginning to take? Do you see that this is nothing more than the fermentation of an idea, an idea that perhaps came to you in the middle of the night, or while you were playing poker, or in the middle of a conversation with a friend? And as the idea became more and more present, became a force of its own, began to speak to you insistently, so much so that you couldn't forget it, you were captured by it, as Tom and I were. You were inspired by it and invigorated by it, so much so that you knew you had to find a way to manifest it in the world.*

*Now, it is completely up to you! Isn't that an extraordinary revelation? That it is yours to do however you are disposed to imagine it? That you, looking at the world from your unique position in the world, get to interpret the needs of the world, and respond to them with the invention you are in the process of creating? This is your opportunity to invent a new world!*

*So, here is my instruction at this point of time in our journey: Take out your "Notes to Myself" and begin to write down whatever, and I mean whatever, comes to mind. Just let it all come out.*

*Write, write, write, to release the flood of impressions you are experiencing, because within that flood is gold from high up on the mountain above you. See it. Feel it. Think about it. Welcome the Thinker, Dreamer! Welcome the Dreamer, Thinker! Pour your heart out onto the page of your life.*

# 15

# Coming to Grips with the Business Model

I gazed gratefully at the ocean. It was so enormous and my
boat was so very small. It could crush me as easily as I
could swat a fly. But it hadn't. It had let me sneak out, get
my fish, and return with nothing worse than a wetting.
What a teacher it was! How much better than the human
teachers with their endless talk about higher
consciousness and the sense and significance of life and
of man. The ocean did not talk of higher consciousness.
But woe betide those who did not watch what they were
doing, who came in or went out carelessly through the
surf, who failed to watch out for the rising of the wind.

—Robert S. de Ropp,
*Warrior's Way: A Twentieth Century Odyssey*

Just as I had struggled and exulted with the pleasure of creating
The Michael Thomas Corporation prior to and after founding it
in 1977, so have I wrestled with the process of inventing In the
Dreaming Room, LLC, prior to and after the day I founded it in 2005.

The process was identical: a Dream is critical to the journey; a
Vision is essential for the Dream to become a reality; this is a Journey,
and like all adventurous journeys, you never know what's going to

happen to you along the way—if you did, it would be called a Trip; and for you to weather this journey, this entrepreneurial odyssey, you need to be passionately invested in creating something remarkable if you are ever going to survive it.

So it was in both my first entrepreneurial venture—The Michael Thomas Corporation, now E-Myth Worldwide—where I learned so many remarkable things; and in my second entrepreneurial venture—In the Dreaming Room—where I learned, and am learning, a whole bunch of stuff my first journey never taught me the confluence of them here in this book will give you a perspective I could never have shared with you until now.

And that is this: Unless your idea for a business exceeds anything you have ever imagined doing before, is bigger than anything you have believed yourself capable of before this moment, has the potential of transforming a large enough number of people's lives in the world to make a huge difference in how the world works, and challenges you sufficiently to risk everything you have to make it a reality, don't do it.

Just don't do it, dear reader, because it will likely disappoint you in too many ways to mention. Don't do it unless you are ready to rumble. Don't do it unless you can put all your fears behind you. Don't do it unless the pain of not doing it will exceed the probable pain of doing it by a factor of ten. Don't do it, because it's not a game one plays casually. Don't do it, because it will confound you, confuse you, threaten to overwhelm you, every single dangerous step of the way.

No, don't do it unless you're ready to stop, then stop again, then look around you and inside of you to ask yourself this very important question: "Am I ready and willing to change the world no matter what might happen to me, so help me God?" And if your answer is a resounding "Yes, yes, yes," then you are an Awakened Entrepreneur worthy of the Journey . . . and you're ready to look at the extraordinary idea of the Perfect Business Model.

▪

A business model simply describes the way a business makes money. For example, you are creating an Internet business that provides information to a certain market segment: people with diabetes, people about to retire, people with capuchin monkeys, people who are serious bicyclists, and because you provide your audience with more information than they could ever hope to find anywhere, they visit your website in droves thirty times a day.

Because of that, the companies who manufacture products or provide services specifically designed for your market segment want to advertise on your website and you are only too willing to let them. It's your business model. That's how you make money. Not by selling information to the visitors of your website, but by selling advertising to the companies that do.

Using the same example, a second business model would be to do the first—attract a large number of capuchin monkey breeders to your website—but instead of selling advertising space to companies who want to sell *their* stuff to capuchin monkey breeders on your website, your intention is to sell *your* stuff directly.

Do you see how the business model changes your perspective? Your "Market" has now become your "Customer" even though they are still the one that all of your attention is focused on: capuchin monkey breeders. Your stuff of course could be anything, including selling space on your website to capuchin monkey breeders to reach other capuchin monkey breeders, and so on.

But, here's the point. Whether your business model calls for selling advertising space to companies who want to reach your market, or for selling your products or services to your Market, now your Customer, really doesn't matter unless you can attract them and keep them coming to your website in droves because they see it as the best place to go for what your Customer/Market perceives they need and can't acquire anywhere else as well as they can from you! And, in both cases in the case above, it is the information you provide—*and the way that you provide it*—that will determine how brilliant your Business Model is or isn't.

Which means to say that:

■ Your Business Model is only as good as your Business Idea, and

■ Your Business Idea is only as good as your determination to do it better than anyone else has ever done it before, or will conceivably do it in the future.

This means that you could provide all the information in the world about anything in the world, but if the way you provide it doesn't successfully differentiate you from all the competition in the mind and heart of your Customer/Market; if it doesn't look, feel, act conclusively different and better than the rest; doesn't compete on price, doesn't stand out as a Brand; and, most important, doesn't produce the result you want and more, then your Business Model sucks, no matter how much sense it makes on the printed page.

In the case above, and any other case you choose, *there is no such thing as the information business. There is only the application business*—the result information produces as opposed to the information itself.

Customers come for results. Customers only come for results. A Business Model that is built on anything other than results is, after all the hurry-scurry at the beginning (think of the dot-com bust), doomed to fail.

Here's an example: the University of Phoenix (UoP). It can easily be demonstrated that the University of Phoenix is not the best place to go for education. Frankly, it doesn't compete in that category. What's more, it doesn't pretend to. If UoP were to try to compete in that category they would fail. No, the University of Phoenix is in the business of providing low-cost, easy-access degrees. They are selling degrees, not education.

UoP doesn't pretend to compete in the education category. Yale, Harvard, Dartmouth, and the like, all compete in the education category. A degree from Harvard is worth significantly more to the graduate of Harvard than a degree from UoP is to their graduates.

To the Customer, the question is not whether the University of Phoenix offers as good an education as Harvard does. The only question is "How do I get a degree at all?" The University of Phoenix is a manufacturer of low-cost, easily acquired degrees that can be earned while continuing in a full-time job. You can't do that at Harvard.

The University of Phoenix's Business Model is priced, delivered, and developed for the Customer who is determined to get a degree he can afford in terms of time and money. The Harvard Business Model is priced, delivered, and developed for Customers who want the very best, exclusive, elite education for their children and can afford to pay for it. The University of Phoenix's customer is not the parent of the student but the student him or herself; a working adult who is determined to get a better job, position, career than the one they can get without a college degree. Again, it's not the education they want, but the degree.

So, obviously, the Business Model is key.

That is why the University of Phoenix is such a brilliant business idea and Business Model. They know what business they are in. They are in the business of providing degrees to people who couldn't get them if it weren't for the University of Phoenix. And so they have developed a perfect model to make the process as painless, as inexpensive, and as productive as they possibly can.

Back to the fundamental question: "What result is your business designed to produce—and for whom?"

And then, "How do you make money doing it?"

■

To Tom and me, The Michael Thomas Corporation was in the business of transforming small business results worldwide by inspiring, teaching, training, and coaching small business owners in the science and art of small business design, implementation, and management.

Our program was to be:

■ Low cost—about the cost of a minimum wage employee
■ Easy to enroll in—only one month's fee in advance, pay as you go
■ Easily accessible—by telephone, fax, mail, and modem.

In short, a service unlike anything our small business owner client had ever been offered before.

What's more, they could enter the program and leave the program at will. In addition, we would demonstrate continually that our program produced increased profit, increased revenue, and increased personal income for our small business owner/client. In addition, our program resulted in decreased stress, increased free time, and increased value of the owner's equity, because we improved the value of his or her business every single time, provided he or she stayed with the program for at least a year. The bottom line is that our program would always produce in results more than the program cost to participate in it.

But—hear me—this is very, very important. All of what I just listed as the benefits of The Michael Thomas Business Development Program were created in our minds and on paper long before we ever produced them! As Tom and I went to work *on* our business (the E-Myth expression of all time), before we ever went to work *in* our business (work *on* it, not *in* it . . . the rest of the story), we committed ourselves to building a program that would produce those very results every single time.

That we *failed* to do it over and over again as we were learning *how* to do it goes without saying. But, because we were *committed* to do it, we *learned* how to do it, and became consistently and incredibly *able* to do it, over and over and over again for tens of thousands of small business clients in 145 countries, clients who came to us without a clue how to do it themselves.

That was our Business Model—to become the no-cost small business development expert worldwide. Not low cost, mind you, but no cost. And by so doing, to transform small business worldwide.

The question, of course, was how could we do that?

What was the "secret sauce," so to speak, that enabled The Michael Thomas Corporation, and now E-Myth Worldwide, to produce such exceptional and predictable results, over and over again for so many small business clients in every imaginable kind of business?

■

I came face-to-face with the very same questions as I began to do Dreaming Room after Dreaming Room. Just as I had gone down the street as our first salesperson, and meeting with clients as our very first business consultant at the beginning of The Michael Thomas Corporation, now, In the Dreaming Room, I was "going down the street" as our very first Dreaming Room Facilitator, facing the same kind of problems—lack of experience, lack of knowledge, lack of understanding—as well as the same kind of breakthroughs: "Oh, so this is what people think of when you mention the word *Dreaming*! Oh, so this is why people resist the entire notion of Dreaming! Oh, this is really, really, difficult to do!"

And each and every Dreaming Room I did challenged the very idea of the business, as well as provided me with every reason to persist with the business.

"What an extraordinary experience this is!" I said to myself as I wrestled with myself and with every participant.

"What a remarkable thing this will be, once I figure it out," I thought.

"But what is the Business Model?" I asked myself continuously.

"It's not, obviously, simply a venue for me to run Dreaming Rooms! Heaven forbid!"

"So, then what?" I asked myself as I doggedly persisted in doing Dreaming Room after Dreaming Room.

"Then what?" appeared as simply as the idea for the Dreaming Room showed up in my mind the first time I thought of it. "Then what?" became so transparently obvious that I wondered why I hadn't seen it at the outset.

"Then what?" was this: The Dreaming Room was not just an intensive weekend workshop. The Dreaming Room was to become "the Power Source for Entrepreneurship Worldwide!"

It was to be a bundled set of services to Awaken the Entrepreneur Within, and then to provide them with all of the inspiration, education, training, coaching, and, most important, the turnkey services they needed to make the job of building a great business easy, affordable, and consistently successful beyond belief. What would those services be?

Here they are:

- MyGrowthPartner.com
- MyGrowthManager.com
- MyGrowthOpportunity.com
- MyGrowthCapital.com
- MyGrowthSoftwareManager.com
- MyGrowthOrganizer.com
- MyGrowthMentor.com
- MyGrowthMarketingEngine.com
- MyGrowthAccountant.com
- MyGrowthAttorney.com
- MyGrowthMedia.com
- MyGrowthAdvertiser.com
- MyGrowthSalesLeader.com
- MyGrowthCoach.com

Each and every turnkey service will provide each and every Awakened Entrepreneur with exactly the kind of help, system, solution, and capability each will need as they go through the stages of entrepreneurial growth, all at the lowest cost possible with the highest probability of success.

The crucial word is *turnkey*.

That is the hallmark of the E-Myth Point of View. The System is the Solution, as my E-Myth books say. When you understand the need for a System, the power of a System, the efficacy of a systems solution to people's problems, then, and only then, can you build a scalable business like McDonald's or Starbucks, or any other business. Only then can you build one turnkey business that works every single time. Only then can you build 30,000 turnkey replicates of that first one—the secret sauce of McDonald's outlandish success. Only then can you ask the question, "Is this business also transformational, in that it will change the world positively from this time on?"

The MyGrowth services are each meticulously based on the turn-key model that McDonald's has so successful built, and, because of that, they provide any and every awakened entrepreneur with the confidence needed to replicate the success of every successful company that is born.

And, by so doing, In the Dreaming Room, the Company will have fulfilled the Dream, Vision, Purpose, and Mission that Tom and I began with The Michael Thomas Corporation: to transform small business worldwide by making certain that every new business in the world is built impeccably, through the utilization of Systems that succeed again and again.

"Just imagine!" I thought to myself as this Vision came to me fully formed and in brilliant color. "Imagine solving the riddle of business failure long before a business is ever built!"

Imagine what it would have meant to Tom and me, long ago, to have had at our disposal turnkey services such as the "My Growth Services."

Imagine if we could have tapped into an intelligent resource, as each of the MyGrowthResources will be, where we could find proven lead generation systems, proven lead conversion systems, proven legal systems, accounting systems, systems for acquiring proven growth managers, capital, partners, professional organizers, systems specialists, and more!

Imagine a huge field of certified solutions, each of which works with all the others in a synchronized manner to produce synchronized results. Imagine being able to acquire all of these services at low cost, and as easily as using the telephone. Imagine providing a website where all of these services and many more could be accessed with the click of a mouse.

Just imagine being connected to every Awakening Entrepreneur in the world, each of whom has participated In the Dreaming Room, each one an active member of Dreaming Groups in which seven Dreamers work together to improve their ability to dream, to vision, to purpose, to mission, to become Masters of Money, to excel at developing their essential skills to build a small company from scratch.

Just imagine that each Group of Seven becomes a part of a Circle of Seven Groups. And each Circle of Seven Groups becomes one of Seven Circles, which make up a World of Entrepreneurs, and each World of Seven Circles makes up a Universe of Seven Worlds. Just imagine that all of these Awakening Entrepreneurs are meeting with one another once a week going through the Dreaming Room Process, telling one another, "I have a Dream, I have a Vision, I have a Purpose, I have a Mission," and getting clearer and clearer as each demonstrates his or her ability to convince the other members of the Group as to the brilliance of their Dream, their Vision, their Purpose, their Mission.

Just imagine that as they develop that ability to articulate their Dream, their Vision, their Purpose, their Mission, they are able to access all of the services they will need to implement their new companies. As they do that, new ventures will spring up all over the world. But they will be ventures with a difference. They will be ventures that *mean* something. And they will be Ventures that will possess the ability to *do what they mean.*

Just imagine a company that could do all that! The Dreaming Room and E-Myth Worldwide and MyGrowthResources all working together with their Strategic Partners, all companies who believe in the Dream, the Vision, the Purpose, the Mission of transforming entrepreneurship worldwide, waking people up to their remarkable potential, teaching people—not only entrepreneurs, but all people—that the gift of dreaming is something that we can all master.

That dreaming, intentional dreaming, as we refer to it In the Dreaming Room, is a gift that will lift all of us on this earth to produce miracles everywhere they are needed.

There is a desperate need for Intentional Dreaming in Africa, where so many struggle with the reality of AIDS, or the lack of clean water, or the knowledge of how to grow healthy foods, or how to run and lead a great country.

There is the same need for Intentional Dreaming in the Middle East, where hate and envy and evil deeds have destroyed lives for decades, if not centuries, but do not need to.

People must begin to see that Dreaming . . . Intentional Dreaming . . . has the power to transform our relationships, and by so doing connect us with one another for the very first time.

Creating new worlds based upon original thinking and dreaming involves a vision, a purpose, and a mission we can all understand. That's because it is not one's vision at the expense of another's, but *one* vision—the ability to create our way out of any circumstance or condition in which we find ourselves.

The business model I envisioned for In the Dreaming Room was both local and global. It was built on the Internet and on the ground. It was available to every single human being through groups, circles, worlds, and universes. Do the math. If there are seven people in every group, and seven groups in every circle, and seven circles in every world, and seven worlds in every universe, there are a total of 2,401 awakened entrepreneurs in just one universe.

If each Dreaming Room market (a geographical designation, such as San Diego) constitutes seven universes of entrepreneurs, that means that San Diego alone has the potential to produce 16,807 awakened entrepreneurs. Sixteen thousand new ventures, all of which work.

Is that possible? "Probably not," replies the Thinker. "Probably not," agrees the Expert. "Probably not," the Cynic echoes. "Probably not," the seasoned veteran of business chips in. "Probably not," says the financial modeler. "Probably not," says your uncle, your brother, your aunt, your father, your mother. "Probably not," says my Dreamer, who is too overwhelmed by the fact of it to become even intrigued by the *possibility* of it.

But, then what? Well, let's just ramp it down a little. Let's just do what everyone who has ever created a stupid business plan does. What if we only got one thousand intentional dreamers to do this thing in San Diego. What if we only enlisted three hundred intentional dreamers to do this thing in San Diego. What about that?

"Oh, screw it!" I said.

"Let's just go ahead and *do it!*" I said.

And so I did. No matter what my uncle, brother, or aunt said.

# STOP
## AND
# FOCUS

# Coming to Grips with the Business Model

The model is the strategic heart of every company. However, it is well that you only sniff it out this early in the game, lest it become the driver of your intention. Your intention is not to build a business model. Your intention is to fulfill your Dream.

Martin Luther King might well have benefited from a business model, as well might the many African Americans he dreamed of serving. But, without his Dream, and the passion that fueled it (or is it the other way around?), his name would not be remembered today, nor would his famous speech, "I Have a Dream."

His Dream was not of a business model, nor did he ever think that way, unless at the core of his thoughts, he might have asked in despair of anyone who was willing to listen, "How are we ever going to get this done?"

That is the second question we've been dealing with here. It is the Thinker's question: "How are you going to get this done?"

It is also the revisit of the question, "What?"

The business model continually bounces back and forth between the two. A strong, focused Thinker is apt to convince the Dreamer that despite the fact that his Vision is not exactly what you had in mind, it's easier to adopt it, and then adapt it, than it would be to press on, and on, and on, trying to figure out how to deliver your Dream with the full force through which you feel it, given how vague it appears to be and how impossible to do.

"Couldn't we just settle down and do this instead?" he is likely to ask. And, of course, your only answer, if you are true to yourself and to me, is "No. But thank you, no."

So, dear, valuable reader, pull out your "Notes to Myself" pad, or whatever you've chosen to call it, and start writing feverishly. We're looking for good stuff here, much like I hope I have shared with you. Push the envelope, go beyond the bland, and discover in your heated rambling an idea worthy of pursuit! Just how the hell are *we going to do this thing we've committed to do?*

# PART FOUR

# THE
# STORYTELLER
## AND
## THE PURPOSE

# 16

# Defining Purpose to Capture Your Imagination

"Perhaps I should not have been a fisherman," he thought.
"But that was the thing that I was born for."

—Ernest Hemingway, *The Old Man and the Sea*

Rick Warren, in his wonderful book, *The Purpose Driven Life*, begins by writing, "It's not about you." The confused, self-centered me would say, "Well, if it's not about me, then who else?" only to find out what Rick Warren meant by the time I got to the second page.

Similarly, this book is not about you. It's about what we are all called to do, if we are called to do anything, that is. This book is about someone hiding in you. It's about the one who creates.

Of course, I have said all this before. I said it when I called this the Age of the New Entrepreneur. I said this when I talked about the Personal Dream as opposed to the Impersonal Dream. I said this when I wrote that entrepreneurs do not create businesses for themselves, they create businesses for others. No self-respecting entrepreneur would create a business for himself or herself. My God, such a business would have only one customer!

I said, too, that most small businesses are *not* invented by entrepreneurs but by technicians suffering from an entrepreneurial seizure who go out and create a business for—whom do you think?—themselves! Why do you think they are miserable? The business is doomed to disappoint them, as a life determined by personal dreams is doomed to disappointment. But we don't know how to do anything else. The only examples we have of people who have done something for someone other than themselves are people such as Mother Teresa, or Gandhi, or Martin Luther King, or perhaps someone you know who has continually lived life for others.

Often, these individuals pay such a price for it! If they don't get killed, they get destroyed by the difficulty of it. If they don't get destroyed by the difficulty of it, they become desperately disillusioned. If they don't get desperately disillusioned, they become hopelessly resigned to living a relatively meager life, without all the benefits that those more self-disposed seem to enjoy.

That raises the question, "Does selflessness, or, put another way, living for other than self, always lead to a life of lack? Is that what you are asking of me, Michael? And why is this so important in a dialogue about entrepreneurship? Do I have to make my life all about a Mission?"

Well, yes and no. But where's the choice?

If someone had a choice between pursuing meaning as a mission, or pursuing self-gratification, what choice would there be? Can you imagine a life without meaning, or, perhaps better stated, a life without purpose? Would you intentionally choose to live a life without purpose? Would you intentionally pursue creating a meaningless business if you had the choice to create one with meaning? A business without meaning would sell meaningless products and services that would satisfy people who live meaningless lives. And how does a business choose meaning over nonmeaning, purpose over lack of purpose? What does all this mean, anyway? Why are we asking so many questions?

▪

It is not just the Dreamer and the Thinker who ask all the questions. The Storyteller does, too. But, the Storyteller's questions are quite different from those asked by those other two, closely aligned as they all are. The Storyteller asks questions that evoke the essence of the Dream, of the Vision, of the Purpose from which all great stories arise, from which all great characters are formed, from which the true magic of the endeavor is inspired.

The Storyteller is the one who sings songs and tells his poetry to anyone who will listen, who writes poetry about the calling, the Dream's intent, the passionate purveyors of the Dream's lyric musing. The Storyteller is the one who captures the Dreamer's heat, the Thinker's logos, and wraps it all into a magical ball that he then throws into the wind.

To catch it as it flies back.

To throw it into the wind again.

To stand in awe of that creativity, which is not limited to artful things, although artful things can be deduced from the simplest beginnings. Even a catcher's mitt can make music, even a belt buckle can sing a song, even a bottle of aspirin can be made to parody a cha-cha. A plain white shirt can become a rabbi's mystical shield against evil, a tricycle can carry an old man to the store to buy groceries, and even a store that sells groceries can become a temple of wisdom if the right person asks the right questions at the right time of the day in the right way.

A great Storyteller need only know the Purpose. When there's a

Purpose, there is a story waiting to be told. If it is a great Story, all the better. The shrewd Storyteller will always rise to the occasion.

■

Every day at The Michael Thomas Corporation was a day to tell our story. I was the one in charge of doing that.

As time went on in those early days and months, it became obvious that I was the Dreamer, Tom was the Thinker, I was the Storyteller, and I was the Leader.

It wasn't that Tom didn't tell the story or that I didn't do any of the thinking. He did and I did. It was simply that he was better suited for so many other things that called for his kind of intellect rather than mine. (I've thought a great deal more about this subject of delegation and the compartmentalizing of accountabilities since, and I'll share it with you in the Leadership part of this book. In short, Tom and I could have done this portion of our partnership much, much better than we did.)

And it was also true that if the Story was to be told I wanted to be the one to tell it. I was always ready to tell the Story. After all, it was I who wrote the Story. And I wrote it in the only way a story gets written: every way and everywhere I could, by telling the story as I went down the street pitching our wares, when a prospect said no and I needed to respond to save the sale, in client meetings when a client didn't understand a recommendation we were making to him, as I led seminars. As I took a shower. As I talked to my wife at night. As I drove to the store. As I walked into the office and out of the office, and while I worked in the office. I wrote the story as Tom and I ate a hurried lunch together in the coffee shop next door.

The story has to be written if the story is going to be told. You can't get around it. But if the story is going to be written, it needs to be told.

First, telling. Then, recording. First saying what comes to you, then recording what came to you. Then memorizing what you wrote down. The process of creating the story for The Michael Thomas Corporation became my personal search for the Holy Grail. And as it became clearer, and the better I could tell it, it became obvious to me that I was telling it everywhere I went, to everyone I met.

I told the story in hiring seminars as we began to hire people.

I told the story in one-on-one interviews as I got to know the people who wanted to come to work for us.

I told the story time and time again to Ellen, the new salesperson I was training to replace me. I told the story to our first consultant, Richard, who was going to replace Tom and me as our only Coach.

I told the story in seminars to dozens of small business owners enrolled by Ellen as we developed our lead generation process so that she could do it as effectively as I could.

I told the story to our banker, to our landlord, when they asked how we were doing, wondering what was going on in there, in the new offices we leased and where new people were showing up every day.

I told the story to my wife, who was wondering why I spent so many hours away from home. I knew I needed to inspire her, to explain it all to her so that she didn't feel so lonely.

And mostly, I told the story to myself, to refine it, to reshape it, to intoxicate myself with it, just like I practiced the saxophone many years before, over and over again, doing the scales, moving my fingers up and down the keys, getting the music down just right, the sound, that extraordinary saxophone sound.

To me, the story was everything.

It wasn't what we did, of course. It was the *story* about what we did.

But had there been no story, had I not immersed myself in the telling of it, what we did would have meant less than nothing. With-out the story about what we did, without telling what our Dream was, what our Vision was, without explaining it in words that rang true, without igniting those words with the passion I felt for what we were doing, without the means through which that passion moved from me into the one to whom I was telling our story, there would have been no transmission from my imagination to their hope. The spirit would have been missing. And if the story is everything, it is the spirit of the story that makes it so.

■

The Story always begins with "Let me tell you who we are and what we do."

When people ask me to describe the Dreaming Room, it is as if I am back there in 1975 all over again, before the Story of The Michael Thomas Corporation had been invented. Back there at the beginning.

Because, even today, months since the very first day of the very first Dreaming Room, the Dreaming Room story is still being written.

But, hey, what the hell, let me tell you who we are and what we do. What follows is the story of In the Dreaming Room. It's the story I tell everyone I meet.

# The Story of the Dreaming Room

*The failure rate of small businesses is horrific.*

*Fully 80 percent of all small businesses fail.*

*Few know the true cost of that failure, but it is staggering when fully understood.*

*Most people who start their own business use savings, personal credit cards, family loans, or a second mortgage on their home to finance their business until it is self-sustaining.*

*Unfortunately, few small businesses are self-sustaining until their third year of operation, which means that the owner often must work a second job to support himself and his family while working in his new business.*

*While he's waiting for his business to grow, the new business owner is distracted by all the things he needs to do and all the things he isn't getting done.*

*The frustrations mount, and the only way he deals with them is to remember the thought that one day when everything is working like a charm he'll be free to take time off, to take vacations with his family, to do the good things a business of your own is supposed to make possible. But, in most cases, the frustrations mount and the "good things" never materialize; not the way he imagined them, that is.*

*(continued)*

*It's then, when the fear that the business will never generate the income he and his family needs, that he begins to feel the real pain of his decision to start a small business of his own. He's terrified that he will never pay down his credit cards, never pay off his second mortgage, and never pay back his family. Just then, when he has just about lost all hope, in walks E-Myth Worldwide, and the business suddenly takes a new direction.*

*And that's fine for the countless millions of operating businesses that need a good dose of what's missing in their business today: leadership, management, marketing, and financial expertise, along with a strong coach who knows how to teach them how to implement that expertise in the development of their business.*

*But, what about all those who are just* thinking *about starting their own business?*

*What would have happened if we had been able to catch our new business owner **before** he made the investment in his new business? **Before** he signed his lease? **Before** he got a second mortgage on his house? **Before** he borrowed money from his family? **Before** he cashed in his savings or his IRA? **Before** he opened a credit line at his bank?*

*What would we tell that potential small business owner who hasn't yet made the decision to start his own business but is just dying to do it? What would we tell him that E-Myth Worldwide isn't telling him now?*

*This is what we would tell him.*

We would tell him that the one thing that's missing in 99 percent of all businesses is a clear and compelling Dream.

It's what great entrepreneurs know that nobody else understands: that a great Dream is essential to building a great business. And a great business is essential if you are ever going to beat the odds of small business failure. It's the only way to succeed.

What's a great Dream?

A great Dream is a great idea for a business that blows people's minds.

A great Dream is what created McDonald's, Starbucks, and Federal Express.

A great Dream is what makes great businesses stand above all the rest.

Imagine living on the edge by creating a stunningly original company, your company, but never feeling overwhelmed, as you would feel without the Dreaming Room, and without your entrepreneurial peers and partners helping you along as you begin to take this new, exciting, incredibly entrepreneurial journey.

At the Dreaming Room, we have invented the power source for entrepreneurship as the only answer of its kind to people who wish to create their own business but do not want to take the outrageous risks such a decision demands.

In the Dreaming Room is the only turnkey entrepreneurial system of its kind.

It helps you to do exactly what you want to do—start a new

(continued)

*business—but without the pain and without the risk, and without the need to make all those painful mistakes that every single new small business owner makes.*

*At the Dreaming Room we are there to inspire you, teach you, train you, and support you every single step of the way. So, how much is it? How much does all that cost? One year in the Dreaming Room costs only $5,000. What do you receive for that?*

*Well, first, a year-long membership with In the Dreaming Room, starting with two and a half intense, creative days working directly with the Dreaming Room's founder and Chief Dreamer, Michael E. Gerber. Second, once you exit the Dreaming Room, we help you to form your own Dreaming Room group with six people you know and want to work with to plan your new company and theirs. There will be seven intentional Dreamers when your group is finally full. Each of those participants will of course come to the Dreaming Room before your group begins in earnest.*

*Next is the support of the Dreaming Room network, and everything it has to offer people just like you throughout the world who are also working the Dreaming Room process to dream and create their own great new business.*

*Not only that, but as a Dreaming Room member you get to revisit the Dreaming Room as many times as you like, provided you bring a new Dreamer with you.*

*Think about it. Only $5,000 and you are ready to fly. So, don't wait. Start now. There is nothing more exciting than beginning to* *dream about your future, knowing that you will never be alone, that you are never on your own, that everything you need to know about building a great new business is just there, waiting, only a website away. Web address www.awakeningtheentrepreneur.com. Call us. Enroll today. Come dream with me!*

# STOP AND FOCUS

## Defining Your Purpose

*What is your Purpose? Do you see now how important the Story-teller is? Do you see why no entrepreneur could be an entrepreneur if he was incapable of telling his story? Of defining his Purpose?*

*What is the importance of what you are doing? What impact will it have on the people your business is being invented to serve? Write a few notes about service. Describe it as though you were talking about service to your little girl or boy. How would you describe being of service to a little child? What words would you use? How would you define it, describe it, discuss it, so that the little child's curiosity was sufficiently piqued, so that the next time you saw him he had questions about it?*

*How do you speak about the urge to serve? Tell a story about it in your place of worship, at the Kiwanis Club, at the YMCA. Tell it at a chamber of commerce breakfast meeting. See yourself saying it: "I woke up one morning with the urge to serve. I had no interest in serving before that moment. I don't know why, or what happened, but I was suddenly called to do something new and different in my life. To find something I could serve to make a difference in the world."*

*That's how a great story begins, it begins inside, inside you, with an inspired moment, a thought, a question, a sudden shift in attention. It starts with a longing, an unrequited urge, a feeling, that something is missing in this picture. Something is missing in your life. It starts in you just like it starts in me. This is the time to pursue it. What is your purpose, what is this great business you are called to create? Take notes, take notes, take notes. This is the time for note taking. Write down, write down, write down everything that arises in you. This is the time to write, write, write. This is the time to pursue your Story.*

# 17

## Pursuing Your Story

The truth is that when his mind was completely gone,
he had the strangest thought any lunatic in the world
ever had, which was that it seemed reasonable and
necessary to him, both for the sake of his honor
and as a service to the nation, to become a knight
errant and travel the world with his armor and his horse
to seek adventures and engage in everything he had read
that knights errant engaged in, righting all manner of
wrongs and, by seizing the opportunity and placing
himself in danger and ending those wrongs,
winning eternal renown and everlasting fame.

—Miguel de Cervantes, *Don Quixote*

I n the Dreaming Room, at the very beginning of the process, people walk in nervously wondering what is going to happen to them.

You can see it on their faces, you can feel it in their bodies, the way they walk, the way they introduce themselves to the people on either side of them, the way they laugh nervously, or the way they stay to themselves.

They are all wearing a question on their sleeve, which is as transparent to me as anything I have ever seen. This question, "What's going to happen to me?" is alive and well and sizzling at the beginning of every Dreaming Room I have ever done.

It sits there inside every person in the room except me.

It sits there like a shadow, like a dark cloud, like a dire prediction, like a dream.

"What's going to happen to me?" is less a question than it is a belief.

But, whatever it is, and however it reveals itself in the moment, it is alive and well at the outset of every Dreaming Room, and will continue to be, I am sure, for as long as I live.

I never thought it would be, but it became quickly apparent to me that this question was at the heart of everything I hoped to accomplish in the Dreaming Room. It would impact the way we were going to connect with one another. The way we were going to discover one another. The way we were going to awaken the entrepreneur within each and every participant in the room before they left.

Remarkably, too, I discovered in retrospect during the dozens of Dreaming Rooms I have done, that this question—"What's going to happen to me?"—is what shaped every small business we had ever worked with at E-Myth Worldwide, and every dysfunctional relationship the owner had had with his or her business, his or her people, and his or her life.

Because this question—"What's going to happen to me?"—was sitting inside every one of our clients as they made their decisions about how big their business was going to be or how small. About how much money they were willing to invest in order to achieve their objectives. About how many people they were willing to hire or how few. About what they were willing to do, and what they were unwilling to do. Every single decision they made and were called to make was driven by the unstated but deeply felt question: "What's going to happen to me?"

Clearly, if anything remarkable was going to happen In the Dreaming Room, it was essential that this question be dealt with at the outset and throughout the two and a half days. Otherwise, all we could expect to happen was more of the same. The business they hoped to create would be no better than the business, or the life, they had created before.

It became obvious to me that this question was the biggest single obstacle standing in the way of every human being on the face of this earth from experiencing true joy.

■

The answer to the question—"What's going to happen to me?"—is very straightforward: "You are going to die."

When I say that, as I always do in the Dreaming Room, everyone laughs.

But not really.

It's that nervous release that pushes the wind out of us in the form of a laugh that's more like a cough, or an uncontrollable hiccup.

It's where I suppose all laughs come from. An instantaneous recognition of the truth told out of context that jars our sensibilities or our sense of composure, the Self that is suddenly put into question.

"Hi, folks, welcome to the truth. We're all going to die. Now that wasn't so bad, was it?"

But, yes, of course it is bad. It's the worst. I don't want to die!

And if everyone in the audience knows they are going to die, then why should everyone be concerned about "What's going to happen to me?" It obviously isn't death everyone is concerned about. We already know we're going to do *that*. We just don't know when. Or how.

Well, that could be what everyone is worrying about . . . *when* they're going to die.

And how they're going to die. Because they don't know *what* death is, what actually happens after we die, the unknown of it is obviously terrifying to anticipate.

Yes, that could be it: fear of the unknown. But my intuition tells me that what everyone is concerned about is, What's going to happen to me between now and the moment I die?

The pain they may have to experience. The loneliness. The suffering. The struggle they may have to endure. The doing without: without money, without comfort, without love, without companionship, without friends, without credibility, without a home, without food, without self-confidence, without control, without . . .

Wait a minute! That sounds like it. *Without control.* Everyone's fear In the Dreaming Room, everyone's fear wherever they are, everyone's fear on the planet is about only one thing: *being out of control.*

Nothing can happen to me that I don't want to happen to me if I retain control.

But, isn't that where the suffering lies? That I know I don't have control? That I know I never have had control? And that every effort in my life has been to try to maximize the control I have over my circumstances? Even then, even when I have tried to maximize the control I have over my circumstances, my experience tells me that I didn't have control, that control was an illusion.

I made decisions without all the information I needed, thinking that I was making the right decisions, thinking that I was in control, only to discover much later that I had left something out.

I wasn't privy to all the information.

I made assumptions based upon faulty or inadequate information.

And then the worst happened. I was suddenly shown that my beliefs, attitudes, and opinions were wrong. And then I experienced the pain, the negative impact of my faulty decisions. I had to make another decision, knowing at the same time that I was possibly going to repeat the same process, because I couldn't be sure that I had all the information I needed, that I didn't possess all the skill I needed, that I didn't possess all the knowledge I needed. But I had to make a decision all the same.

And the habit of fear set in. That fear now lives inside me, no matter how little I might notice it, to color every decision I make from this time forward: "What's going to happen to me, what's going to happen to me, what's going to happen to me?" becomes the refrain that regulates my life.

But, at least in this life, I know I'll get another chance to do it again.

But, in whatever follows death, who knows where I'll be, all alone. And is it dark there? And what does the word "control" mean in a world where I don't have any at all?

▪

So, the terror of our situation comes forcefully into the present In the Dreaming Room.

Not because I call it in, but because you walk it in with you.

It's been with you every second of your life from the very beginning when you were just a little kid doing what kids do, learning what kids learn, dreaming about what kids dream about. Long before you learned the lessons that posed the question "What's going to happen to me?" because you discovered first that you were someone to whom things happened.

That was a big one, wasn't it? First, you were a part of everything and everything was a part of you, and then, moment by living moment, you became acculturated to the human fact that you were a separate self, an identity that had borders, that there was an inside and an outside. You were inside, and everything and everyone else was outside. And things came in from the outside to disrupt the inside. And you began to be wary of the outside stuff because it wasn't always pleasant on the inside. You began to live with the need to control the outside so as to control the inside. That became your method for growing up in the dangerous world you were born into.

To some of us, that happens very, very early. To some of us, that happens later. But it happens to every single one of us sooner or later and is now known famously as the Human Condition.

■

So, each participant walks into the Dreaming Room with a wish to change that condition, usually without having thought about it the way I am describing it here. Unfortunately, the condition cannot change until we are aware of it.

That is what happens in the Dreaming Room.

The Dreaming Room process makes each participant aware of the human condition as it manifests itself in them in the choices they have made in their lives, and how the way they made those choices is playing itself out right here in the Dreaming Room as they are attempting to start their life all over again.

You can't get *there* from *here*, if *here* is where you are as a result of all the choices you have made, and if *there* is where you would prefer to be if life would allow you.

In the Dreaming Room is where all of that stops. "All of that stops" means that for each and every participant In the Dreaming Room we begin anew by playing games. Yes, games. They have names like "A Blank Piece of Paper and Beginner's Mind," "Stop!" "We're Not Here to Fix OldCo, We're Here to Invent NewCo," "You're

About to Invent a New Business," and "You're About to Invent a New Life."

■

So, that's a piece of my Story.

Now, as we move forward together, what is *your* Story?

What is it you're here to do? What do you need to do to discover it? How do you begin *your* life anew?

# STOP AND FOCUS

## Pursuing Your Story

*This is a sacred moment. This is where you begin in earnest to discover the Story that will forever change the trajectory of your life. This is that big moment, that significant moment, that momentous moment. In this moment, as you sit here reading these words of mine, your life is being called into question. Call it. Don't engage in this dialogue with me passively, but actively.*

*Imagine that I am going to be your guide, I am here to serve you, I am here to engage you in a new process unlike anything you have ever done before. The inside and the outside strategy that has engineered your life to this moment will become a thing of the past. The Way ahead is clearly different from the Way that brought you here.*

*Is this spiritual work? Yes and no. It is to the degree we all are spiritual beings. But it isn't, to the degree that there is no tradition we are going to follow, there is no belief we have to subscribe to, and there is no ritual I will ask you to master. There is only you and there is only me, and there is the entrepreneur within each one of us who is awakening to invent something that calls for all of our available energy, all of our imagination, all of our passion and creativity reserved for the creation of the outside that is a product of our inside, and in the process they form the one thing we are all here to be.*

*We are what we think. We are what we do. We are who imagines. We are that which we imagine, and that which we imagine is who we are. "I am," said the one. I am, I say to you. And you are that, too. Let's go on to envision the Story. The Story you are here to create. The Story that is you.*

■

# 18

## And the Story Grows from Within

Songwriting is about getting the demon out of me.
It's like being possessed. You try to go to sleep,
but the song won't let you. So you have to get up and
make it into something, and then you're allowed to sleep.
It's always in the middle of the bloody night, or when
you're half-awake or tired, when your critical faculties are
switched off. So letting go is what the whole game is.

—John Lennon

I am certain that the Google boys knew—and know—their story. I am certain that Bill Gates knew and knows his, too. I am certain that Frank Lloyd Wright knew his story. And that Gandhi did, too. I am certain Picasso knew his story, and Einstein did, as well. I am certain that George Washington and Benjamin Franklin knew their stories, as did Mother Teresa.

I am certain that every single one of the men and women who championed something of significance in their life knew their story cold, and that their lives were a projection of that story. They were there to infuse their story with their vitality, to manifest their story in any way they could.

That is what the hierarchy of humanity is to me. These are the sort of things one is inspired by, these very human things, until the time we become inspired by something even higher than that. The Something we know to be God. The something we know to be the ineffable. The something we know to be the Unknowable.

These things I speak about, these human things, these products of our imagination are of course not the highest that we can aspire to, but they are, nonetheless, the most inspired things we can do. In this world. At our state of being. They are the most inspired things we can do, given the human condition.

We can aspire to give joy to other human souls. We can aspire to reach beyond our human condition. We can aspire to create a world of human abundance, a world in which commercial activity can be fused with the world of spiritual activity to become inspired activity beyond that which our spiritual leaders and our commercial leaders have discovered on their own. We can aspire to merge the best with the best so that the worst we do is better than anything we have ever done before.

What would happen if the passion of Dr. Martin Luther King, Jr., could have been joined with the tenacious brilliance of Bill Gates? What would happen if you had joined the profound dedication of Mother Teresa with the playful imagination of Steve Jobs? What would happen if you could have joined the creative force of Walt Disney with the creative genius of Picasso? What would happen if you joined these two worlds, the commercial and the spiritual, to create spiritually charged economic success? What would the impact of that be?

Welcome to the Age of the New Entrepreneur! We have seen it, we have tasted it, we have begun it, and I can say with the supreme confidence of a very practical man, that it's all over but for the shouting. Welcome to the Dreaming Room.

▪

You begin to pursue your Story wherever you are, exactly as I did. There is nothing I have done that you can't do. There is nothing I can do that you can't do as well, or better than I. Nothing. I have said it before: "I have done it, and so can you!" You begin it exactly where you are, not where you're not. You begin it right here, right now. Come with me as we seriously begin the journey. Start writing after me.

> *I want to create a world of meaning. I want to contribute to that by inventing a new business prototype that will exceed anything I have ever done. It will do what it does exactly as I perceive it. It will be a business of meaning. It will produce cash flow from the very beginning in excess of what it costs to produce that cash flow.*
>
> *This business I am inventing will make a demonstrable difference in people's lives. I will make that difference the point of my Story. My Story will describe that business to a T. People will say when they hear my Story, "Wow, how do you do that?" And I will tell them exactly how we do that. But even more important, I will tell them why we do that.*
>
> *My Story will get better and better each time I tell it. It will become the passion that fuels my life. I will see myself as a leader in the world of people making a difference in the world. I will seek out those people who make a difference in the world to tell them my Story, and to ask them to tell me theirs. I will seek out great Stories every day and in every way possible. I will build a personal library of great Stories and read one of them*

*at the beginning of every day and at the end of every day to fuel my life with their passion.*

*I am a writer of great Stories. I believe in the power of great Stories. I believe in the power of great Stories as they are told by great teachers of great Stories. I am dedicated to becoming a great author of my great Story and a great teacher of great Stories, mine and every other great teacher's great Story.*

*I live to inspire human beings to live great lives. I am committed to the Path of Greatness not for myself, but for those who will be profoundly affected by it. For those who will follow me on that path. For those who are hurting for want of a great Story, a great path, a great calling. I will create such a great path, such a great Story, such a great calling as I write my great Story, as I invent my great path.*

*I envision a world of great warriors. Inner warriors, not outer warriors. Inner warriors who are equally committed to the Great Path. Inner warriors who are committed to leading the Great Life. Inner warriors who are committed to write their great Story, to tell their great Story, to create their great path, to live the great life, the life of a great warrior.*

I have written this for *you*. I have invited you with this book to join me in the creation of my great Story by creating your great Story as we all create the great story of all Stories of all time.

The world will never be the same, brothers and sisters. The world will not challenge us. The world will greet us, harbor us, feed us, nurture us, and inspire us, because the world is a great Story—the greatest Story of all.

# STOP
## AND
# FOCUS

## And the Story Grows from Within

*Are you beginning to feel the urgency of all this? The urgency to awaken the One within you who wishes to write, to speak? Who wishes to discover his or her voice? The One who is tired of not singing? The One who is tired of not creating? The One who is tired of watching you work for a living? The One who is tired of being suppressed? Who is tired of not being heard?*

*How is it that everyone can have a Story but you? How is it that with all that is destroying the world there are no easy Stories just lying around waiting for someone to see them, hear them, want them, respond to them?*

*These Stories I speak of are everywhere you look! There are people struggling who do not have to struggle. There are people striving who do not have to strive so hard. There are people who have eyes, but cannot see. Ears, but cannot hear. Feelings, but cannot feel. These people are everywhere. Over six billion of them.*

*They do without. They will always do without until the entre-preneur within you awakens to their lack, to their longing, to their pain, to their frustrations.*

*Let me say it again . . . these people are everywhere you look.*

*(continued)*

*All you need to do is look. To watch them and get to know them. That's where your Great Story is. Was I the only one who saw the struggle in small business worldwide? Could I have been the only one who said, "Why, there is absolutely no reason these people have to work so hard for so little. There is absolutely no reason why most small businesses should fail. None whatsoever. So, what is the problem? What is it all those small business owners can't see? What is it that is standing perpetually in their way?"*

■

*After all is said and done, you are the only one who is going to make this Story come true. You are going to make the decision to either create a Great Story or not. It all comes back to you.*

*You are following this Path, and I want to remind you that while I am loving the Story we are creating together, I know, and have known, all the time that we've been doing it, that there is an unspoken truth that must be spoken if we are ever going to strike pay dirt: you are being called to make a commitment. It won't happen without you. Your contribution to the world will not happen without you. Your invention will not be invented without you. Your participation in the awakening of your entrepreneur will not happen without you.*

*You, when it finally comes down to it, are the master of this entire collection of I's within you. The ones we're calling forth: the Dreamer, the Thinker, the Storyteller, the Leader. They all depend upon you. They all are looking to you and asking the unasked, but* ever-present question, which is, "Are we going to do this thing? Is it a go?" For the Story to be told, you must tell it. For the Mission to unfold, you must lead it. For the risks to be taken, you must risk it. For the journey to be continued, you must continue it. For the Mission to be accomplished, you must accomplish it.

With each and every Story from the Dreaming Room there was a Peter and an Elena and a Rick who had to commit, to put themselves on the line, who had to actually go out there and do it. Every single one of them came to the Dreaming Room feeling very much like you right at this moment. The Stories I am sharing with you here, and the way I am sharing them—the actual writing of this book!—are all from real life, the kind of life you are living. You, not your entrepreneur, not your Dreamer, your Thinker, your Storyteller, your Leader, but you. This is your Story.

Where we sit right now with this book in your hands, this is your Story we are talking about. You get to claim it for yourself. You get to chart the course. You get to physically write it, to speak it, to do it, to make it come alive. So, please, take out your notebook and write this down lest you forget it: This is for me to do. This is only for me to do. This is mine. This is my own Path. I create it. I live it. I proclaim it to be mine. This is my singular place to be on this earth. Write it. Take it in. It is true.

# PART FIVE

# THE LEADER

## AND

# THE MISSION

# 19

# The Leader

The most important thing in the world, implies wisdom
master Nachman of Bratzlav, is to be willing to give up who
you are for who you might become. He calls this process the
giving up of *pnimi* for *makkif*. For Master Nachman, pnimi
means the old familiar things that you hold onto even
when they no longer serve you on your journey, makkif
is that which is beyond you, which you can reach only
if you are willing to take a leap into the abyss.

—Marc Gafni, *The Mystery of Love*

I've talked about the Leader in all of my *E-Myth* books, most specifically in my most recent *E-Myth* book, *E-Myth Mastery: The
Seven Essential Disciplines for Building a World Class Company.*

I've talked about the five essential skills needed to lead anything
of significance: the skills of Concentration, Discrimination, Organization, Innovation, and Communication.

I've talked about the difference between the Marketing Leader,
the Financial Leader, the Management Leader, and the Leader of the
Enterprise.

Here, however, I want to discuss the Leader from a completely
different perspective. Now I want to talk about leadership *before* the

company has been created. At the blank piece of paper Stage of Leadership.

Blank, however, with several caveats:

- The Dreamer, the Thinker, the Storyteller have each done their jobs well.
- There is a Dream in place, as well as a Vision and a Purpose, all ready to define the Mission.
- A lot of thinking has been done to provide the logic for the Mission sufficient to generate a passionate commitment from the Leader to take it on.
- The Story has legs.
- It is a moving Story.
- The Leader is confident not only that he or she can tell the Story, but that he or she is excited about telling it.

■

Let's examine how this works. I will do that by taking you through a conversation I might have with just such a Leader. It could even be a conversation I would have with myself, or it might be with someone I intend to recruit to take on the accountability of this incredible company I am in the process of creating—a company we are calling *Who Is Manny Espinosa?*

*Who Is Manny Espinosa?* is a fictitious company (for now) in the business of recruiting and developing young Latinos between the ages of seventeen and twenty-four for the purpose of preparing them for entry-level positions in the restaurant, hospitality, and construction industries, where new employee attrition averages an outrageous 100 percent per year.

That means that the restaurant industry in the United States loses 250,000 employees per week, for a total of approximately 12 million employees per year. Since the restaurant industry only employs a total of 12 million people, an increasing number of whom are Hispanic, that means, technically, the industry is losing the equivalent of all of its employees each and every year! Astonishing, isn't it?

Well, that's the problem *Who Is Manny Espinosa?* intends to solve. How? By teaching many young Hispanics the street skills, business skills, and life skills nobody has ever taught them before.

The restaurant, hospitality, and construction industries will then become the customers of *Who Is Manny Espinosa?* because we will become the provider of choice for all new employees for those industries. We will become that because, through our unique intensive training and support programs, the young workers we provide to those industries will stay on the job longer, be more productive, and be more likely to become managers than any entry-level employees those industries have hired before.

Understand, this COO (Chief Operating Officer) I am interviewing is a fictional character (for now!), not a real one. My intention is not to bore you with my history, but to intrigue you by looking at yours before you create it!

So, play the game with me. Remember, we are talking about leadership here. That Leader is either you or someone you are going to entrust with your financial and creative future. We are about to make one of the most important decisions any entrepreneur will ever have to make: the selection of a Leader to lead his or her enterprise.

■

## MEETING THE LEADER

Who is this person sitting in front of me? What motivates him? Why does he feel this is the opportunity he has been seeking? Or does he? Who is he really? What is he *really* thinking?

I'm sitting in front of a finalist for the COO position of my new company, *Who Is Manny Espinosa?*, and I'm about to find out the answers to these questions.

The candidate is a man in his early fifties. He's athletic looking, clear eyes, about 6'1", looks to be about 180 pounds. He is a lean man, neatly groomed, with a perpetual look of curiosity on his face . . . like he is wondering just where this meeting is going to take us. He is probably thinking the same about me: "Who is this man, Michael Gerber, really? Can I trust him? Does he know what he's doing? Is this company going to realize its ambitions? Do I want to work for him? Can I depend upon him to keep his word?"

His name is John Blackwell. He was brought to me by an executive search firm I retained for the very first time in mid-July 2007. I had had a tumultuous relationship with a previous executive search firm, in that my expectations of the executive manager I was looking for weren't met by the firm, and it cost me a lot of money and time to correct the problem. So, I was wary when I began this process all over again.

My problem the first time was caused by me.

I wasn't clear enough in communicating my needs to the candidates they brought me.

I wanted someone to be my COO; they convinced me that we would have much greater success if we looked for a CEO candidate reporting to me. I would be chairman of the board.

I acquiesced because I didn't know any better. In retrospect, I would never do that again. While the CEO position was much easier for the recruiter to fill, the COO position was critical, especially at this stage of the company's launch. I didn't intend to hand over my new venture to someone else to lead. I had done that before and it proved a disaster. Now I intended to lead it myself while delegating the secondary leadership role to someone who lived for and thrived on execution, who loved to make ideas come to life in the operation of a company. Someone whose past history demonstrated he or she could implement strategy in the day-to-day reality of a company for a CEO who possessed a worthy vision and exhibited the passion and personal magnitude necessary to inspire customers to buy, employees to buy in, suppliers to support the company's growth commitments, and investors who bought into the company's Story just as the CEO had shared it with them.

In short, the COO was someone who could be a strong right-hand kind of guy, a great translator of the company's Story for those who needed to be inspired by it if the job the company had been assigned to fulfill would be done.

The COO needed to demonstrate in his behavior that the Story was not just the CEO's Story, but his Story as well. He would not be a sycophant, but would rather be a man who could take on the Mission they were there to pursue because the Mission would mean something to him. It would move him and bring out the best in him. He would be committed to it, and that was why he was here . . . to make the Mission happen without fail.

John Blackwell appeared to be just that guy. But, of course, even though we had had several meetings and covered everything anyone would need to know in order to make a career decision, we were just beginning the real conversation. The conversation that would either satisfy me that John Blackwell was the guy I was looking for, or not. As I said, I had made the mistake before, believing that what the CEO candidate was saying was what the CEO candidate was actually feeling. Foolish me. This time I needed to do it right. There was little time, room, or money available for me to make another mistake.

John Blackwell knew of my concerns. He went on to address them in the following way.

"Michael, there's a saying in my family, my dad's saying actually, which goes something like this: 'Do not take on anything you will live to regret. And do not regret anything you have taken on.' Which meant to my dad that there's no room for sloppy thinking, either before you make a commitment or after you've made one. I never take on anything I am not going to see through. It doesn't mean I am infallible. My father never expected that of any of us, nor did he humor arrogance in any of his kids. But, what he essentially said is that commitments are the most honorable part of being human. They are never to be taken lightly. They are for good."

John Blackwell paused thoughtfully, and then continued.

"I've listened carefully to what you intend to accomplish with *Manny Espinosa,* the company, but I still have a number of questions I need to ask to understand it the way I need to in order to take it on.

"The first question is about Manny himself. Why is he important to you? What makes you think you can make a difference in his life, when so few others have? In other words, what do you know about him that nobody else seems to?"

My answer was quick and to the point. "Actually, I have no reason to believe I know more about Manny than anyone else does, nor about what it's going to take for our company to make the difference we intend to make. All I know is that I'm committed to do it simply because it needs to be done. Everything I've learned about Manny tells me his life sucks. And my intuition and my experience tell me that I can find the people who know what we need to know to change that, and that I can inspire the right people to make it happen. I feel that in every bone in my body. There's no doubt in my mind that it will be done. If not by me, by somebody. And I intend for us to be the one."

John Blackwell smiled as I finished. "But why are you so committed to do it, Michael? You've already got just about everything anyone needs to make you happy. You've built a successful company. You've achieved a certain level of notoriety. You've had a significant impact on the world of small businesses, and the people who run them. And you're seventy years old. Why aren't you retiring? What do you need this for?"

I smiled in response to his question. It was a great one—one that just about everybody asked me. The answer was also a simple and straightforward one.

"I need to, John, simply because I love the challenge of it. Here's an opportunity to do something meaningful. Something that, if we do it incredibly well, could literally transform the lives of millions of people, the communities they live in, their families and their families' families, and entire industries as well. It's simple because it's so big. It's exciting because it's so impossible. It's important to me because it's fun to think about, to talk about, and, despite how difficult it might be to actually pull it off, it will be more fun to do than to just think about doing it. Imagine the impact this could have on the entire country if we pull it off. We're talking about a growing population of many millions of kids whose lives are mostly off track, an entire generation of people. To be honest, I can't imagine *not* doing it. Does that answer your question?"

John nodded yes, and then said, "Then let me ask you this: If I prove to be the best candidate for this position, how free am I to do it the way I think it needs to be done? How much control do you intend to exercise over your COO?"

"Great question, John," I replied. "The answer is not so simple as the last two I gave you, but let me give it a try." I felt myself tightening up a bit for fear that I wouldn't be as direct as I needed to be if I were to be totally honest with him. This is where I had screwed up the last time. But I needed to do this, so I continued to say what needed to be said.

"I described to you the look of the company as I envision it, as well as the feel of it and how it would represent itself to the people it needs to impress. I also talked about the way it would act and the financial results it would need to deliver. What I didn't say is that each of these categories—the Visual, Emotional, Functional, and Financial measures of the company—are incredibly important to me. More than you probably would expect. There are standards for each and every company I want to create. Every company, not just this company. To me, the way I described them to you is not just a wish, but a serious expectation. Call it a mandate.

"So, everything you do as COO of *Manny Espinosa* must be done in a way that is completely consistent with those standards. My standards. There is no flexibility whatsoever when it comes to them. There will be a dress code, for example, and that dress code will be followed exactly, by everyone in the company, just like a Marine in his dress blues would . . . impeccably.

"*Impeccable* is an important word to me, John. It means in accordance with the highest standards. I can see when a thing is done impeccably, and I can see when it's not. So can you, if it is important enough to you to look and to care about it like I do. I can't give that to you, it has to live in you if it's going to be important to you. My expectation is that *Manny Espinosa,* the Company, will be impeccable in everything it does. The COO who leads it forward will not only honor that Vision, but will live that Vision. *How* you do that is of course your decision. *That* you do that, however, is a hard and fast agreement between us. Of course, I will try to influence your decisions every chance I get. And at the beginning of our relationship, I'm sure that we'll get into quite a few tussles about it. But, in the end we'll have come to agreement about most things, sometimes in your favor, sometimes in mine. But always in accordance with the rules of the game we establish between us.

"I understand how difficult that might be for you. For example, everyone has his or her opinion about dress codes. But their opinions don't matter to me. Only my opinion does. I believe in dress codes. I believe in impeccability. I believe they communicate both solidarity and tradition. I believe they say something about the integrity of the organization that differentiates it from just any organization.

"That's just one of the requirements or standards I would expect you to meet. And of course it is critical to me that you do not fulfill a standard of mine unless you completely believe in it. If you don't believe in it, but still honor it, we will eventually come to an impasse. I know that, because I've experienced that, and I'm unwilling to experience it again."

I continued. "Another standard of mine, and therefore of *Manny Espinosa*, the Company, is that of Systems. Everything we do will be documented as a system. Implemented as a system. And those systems will become a significant part of our operating mind-set. And the systems have to mean something to our people and to the people we work with—the Manny Espinosas we will be training and developing into Leaders in their communities, and the cadre who train them. To me, the System we employ stands for impeccability, authority, consistency, and order. It says that we have the ability to figure out how to do anything we set our minds to do, and that when we figure it out we will systematize it into the very fabric of our company so that anyone, no matter who, can use that system with impunity to produce the results we're here to produce for all the Mannys we train and develop and all the companies we place them with.

"What that says to me is that we can show Manny how to become incredibly effective at whatever he decides to do, provided he figures out the system through which to do it. We will show him that figuring out the system takes concentration, discrimination, organization, innovation, and communication skills that he must learn to use and develop, to internalize for the development of his or her life. And that we can teach him or her exactly how to do it. That makes us his very best friend, because nobody else in his life is teaching him that, or will teach him that, because no one in his life has become a master of that the way we will be. Since that is our commitment to Manny, it is your job as COO to lead that initiative within our company to make that mind-set a living, disciplined, and heartfelt reality in every single thing we are called to do, or intend to do.

"In other words, John, as the operational Leader of *Manny Espinosa,* the Company, you must become the exemplar of every trait, standard, and belief the company espouses to every Manny we take on for as long as you're here. It's more a life role than it is a job. Again, *how* you do that is your call. *That* you do that is mine. Does that answer your question?"

John Blackwell nodded again in agreement, but not, I thought, as a sycophant would. He seemed earnestly interested in what I was saying, as though I wasn't saying anything other than what made sense to him.

He responded, "The conversation we're having reminds me of several that I had with my father. He taught me that I honored myself in the process of taking serious things seriously. By devoting myself to them, I honored them, and I honored the process they represented. So, when you tell me what is important to you, Michael, if I don't understand why it is important to you, I will ask you why it is, and once I understand why it is, I will give you my word that I will honor your standards as if they were mine. Once I understand and come to agreement with those standards, they will be mine. And when they become mine I will live them completely with every fiber of my being. So, as the saying goes, be careful what you wish for because you might get it. With me, you can be certain you will get it."

John Blackwell paused for a moment and then said, "So, here's my final question. When do we start?"

"Not until we're clear about my other expectations," I answered.

■

The Leader of your company must not only agree with your Dream, Vision, Purpose, and Mission, he or she must be enthralled with it.

He or she must be of the type who believes in ideas, and doesn't just give lip service to them.

The greater the idea, the better.

A supposed Leader I had contemplated moving up in my company once said about my books, "They're only books, Michael." Now understand me, they happened to be *my* books, but that wasn't what decided it for me with this person. It was his attitude about ideas, which is what of course a book is, a set of ideas communicated in a story.

What he was really saying to me was that they were only ideas. They were only words, which to me meant that ideas were not important to him. How could I possibly put my company into the hands of a person to whom ideas were unimportant, when to me ideas are the most important of all things when it comes to creating a company? The ideas that form the idea (core) of the company are also the ideas that inspire the people in your company to commit themselves to the fulfillment and realization of those ideas. Your Leader must embrace those ideas with his or her whole being.

After all, the United States Constitution is only a set of ideas, but those ideas form the core belief systems that underlie the formation and experience of living in this country.

The Bill of Rights is a document of ideas. Without those rights, which are themselves ideas, we would not be the country we are today. Without those rights, there would be no laws, and without those laws, which are only ideas, there could be no justice in the country we live in.

So, it is critical that the Leader within the Entrepreneur, or in service to the Entrepreneur for whom he has elected to lead, must agree with the Entrepreneur's ideas. And to agree with them, he or she must be interested in them, pursue an understanding of them, and then commit himself or herself to them in the fulfillment of his or her accountabilities.

■

I then provided John Blackwell with a list of my core leadership beliefs. There were, and still are, ten:

1. Lead with Purpose, commit yourself to your Mission.
2. Once committed, never alter your commitment until you have achieved it.
3. Create clear operating standards, and live by them.
4. Create clear operating results, and commit to them.
5. Surround yourself with people who believe in your Mission.
6. Surround yourself with people who are committed to your Mission.
7. Surround yourself with people who believe in your standards.
8. Surround yourself with people who are committed to your standards.
9. Surround yourself with people who are committed to your results.
10. Surround yourself with people who are faithful to their commitments.

I then went on to share with John Blackwell my other operating standards related to the fulfillment of his accountabilities.

1. Learn how to produce results with little or no capital.
2. Learn how to produce results with little or no information.
3. Learn how to produce results with little or no experience.
4. Learn how to produce results with little or no likelihood of success.
5. Learn how to do the impossible.
6. Learn how to inspire people without money, without motivation, without options.
7. Learn how to manage people without making them wrong.
8. Learn how to communicate your Dream, Vision, Purpose, and Mission so that 90 percent of the people you share it with buy into it. Do not spend any time with the 10 percent who don't.
9. Learn how to replicate your successes and rise above your failures.
10. Learn how to become a world-class Leader you can be proud of.

And then, after three days more of talking and going deeper and deeper into the conversation and the implications of it, I said to John Blackwell, "So, *now* what do you think of this opportunity? Still want to get started?"

And John Blackwell said, "Yes. Most certainly."

And we did.

# STOP AND FOCUS

## The Leader

As you read the previous interview with John Blackwell, it could well be productive if you were to have that interview with yourself. How would you have responded to my questions, my mandate, and my requirements for the position of Chief Operating Officer? Did you feel that my needs were too intrusive, that I was expecting too much from him, that I was being unrealistic?

Did you feel that John was too agreeable, not challenging enough, too willing to be my right-hand guy? Was he assertive enough? On the other hand, could you understand why I was so determined to make certain that he had the right stuff I believed I needed to run the company the way I wanted it run?

Imagine interviewing the Leader in you, the one who is going to take on the responsibility for fulfilling your Mission. How tough do you need yourself to be? How dedicated? How articulate do you imagine you will need to be to tell the Story of your emerging new company to all members of the community who need to be enrolled continuously in what your company is there to do? Look inside and ask yourself if you're ready to take on John Blackwell's job. And what exactly is his job?

Well, of course he needs to be a master of money. He needs to understand cash flow, the balance sheet, and the income statement. He needs to understand budgeting and financial forecasting. He *needs to have a tight control over expenditures against plan, and plan against new contingencies.*

*He also needs to know people—how to recruit them, hire them, fire them when need be, develop them into Leaders, monitor and review their performance, know when to change their roles in the company, and develop standards of performance by which they'll be measured.*

*He needs to know marketing and lead generation and client fulfillment. He needs to know how to develop a winning relationship with his customers as well as with community influences, parents, government, local business organizations like chambers of commerce, Kiwanis, Rotary, and all of the Latino organizations that might impact positively or negatively Manny's relationship with* Manny Espinosa, *the Company.*

*Of course, John Blackwell, the Leader in you, also must develop a deep understanding of your primary customer, Manny, himself/herself. Your Leader needs to accomplish all of this in a normal eight-hour day, while looking great, acting with authority, and growing the company for which he is accountable.*

*If that weren't enough, John Blackwell, the Leader within you, needs to create the Mission's Plan, and then implement it.*

*Welcome to the Leader. Welcome to the world of work. Welcome to what must happen today if the Dream is to become a reality. Are you ready yet?*

# 20

## The Leader Goes to Work

*Meaning has no meaning apart from intention.*
—Rollo May, *Love and Will*

There is a clear path to inventing a new company, and there is a muddy path. The muddy path looks just like it sounds— muddy. There is no order. Stuff happens, and stuff gets done, or it doesn't, but the people in the business are so busy with their stuff that they have no energy, time, or interest for anyone else's stuff. And of course they can rationalize it, because, after all, that's the nature of a new business. Everything is so new that no one has any experience that can exactly correlate with it, so you're making stuff up as quickly as you can just to keep the boat afloat. And somehow stuff gets done.

Or, as I said a moment ago, it doesn't.

John Blackwell's Mission, your leader's Mission, is fortunately quite different.

John Blackwell has entered a phase in the business creation process where his mandate is to think very, very small.

His job is to build the DNA of the enterprise. That's as important a task as there is at this stage. This is what I mean by building the DNA of the enterprise:

In E-Myth terms, I have described a Company as a hierarchy of three. The lowest level in the hierarchy is the DNA of the hierarchy. It is called the Practice. A Practice is the simplest completely self-sufficient operating unit of the company. It includes the three essential systems of Lead Generation, Lead Conversion, and Client Fulfillment. These three are required for the Company to produce income and grow. These systems are then developed until they perform in a predictably effective manner, are documented, and are transferable with minimal training to relatively low-level employees. This then becomes the Expert Operating System, the Core Competence that enables the Practice to be scaled exponentially to deliver its unique and highly differentiated capability to its customer. This DNA is the heart of a Company's Brand.

I call the next level of the hierarchy the Business. The Business is nothing more than an aggregate of multiple Practices, each a replicate of the very first one, plus a Business Management System (BMS) that enables the Manager of the Business to monitor, control, and improve the operating systems comprising the Practices for which he is accountable. The job now is to develop, improve, and perfect the Business Management System so that the Business can be scaled.

The third stage of the Company's hierarchy is the Enterprise. The Enterprise is the aggregate of multiple Businesses (Districts), each utilizing the expert Business Management System through which the multiple Practices in each Business are effectively managed and continually improved.

A Leadership System is developed within the Enterprise, the purpose of which is to lead the management of the Businesses toward greater productivity through inspiration, education, application/ training, coaching, and consulting. These five essential functions are also critical for the managers of the Businesses to utilize in their development of the people within each Practice.

Finally, and as the company grows, there will be multiple Enterprises (Regions), which will operate identically, built on exactly the model just presented here. When a large organization is built in this manner, the consistency of systems and the people who utilize them can be more readily engineered to produce a consistent result for all influences within the Company as well as without. This is how Wal-Mart was built, how McDonald's was built, how Starbucks was built, and how Dell computer was built. From the ground up.

This is John Blackwell's Mission. This is your Mission as well.

This, fortunately, is also the golden goose that lays the golden eggs for anyone who desires to invent a remarkably successful enterprise. This is what awakens the entrepreneur within. It's the sudden realization that any one of us can conceive of a Practice, design that Practice, build that Practice, perfect that Practice, and replicate that Practice to produce inconceivable results, all with little investment capital at the beginning, and only a great idea to fuel your imagination and your ability to grow.

Welcome to the Age of the New Entrepreneur where anything has just become possible for anyone who can conceive it!

# STOP
### AND
# FOCUS

## The Leader Goes to Work

*"The Golden Goose That Lays the Golden Eggs!" Do you truly recognize the liberation of it? We have just at this moment come to the inescapable, unavoidable, irrepressible joyful truth of it . . . that with little more than a Great Idea, a Great Business Model, and a Great Story, you can conceive, design, build, perfect, and roll out your own McDonald's. You can create your own perfectly wonderful, meaningful Enterprise, and you can start doing it today with your own powerful Mission.*

*The System is already there, my friend! And it's turnkey. All you need to do is apply it to your Great Idea, persist as you lead it forward, do as John Blackwell is committed to doing, as I have, and as so many millions of others have, are, and will.*

*It's time to create a revolutionary new world. Go back now to the beginning, dear reader. Go back to all of your notes. Begin taking yourself seriously. Now that you see how simple this is going to be, go back and read your Great Story. Didn't write it yet? Then begin. Now. Before you forget how easy this is.*

*Do you see that there is no longer any reason that you can't do it? It is not the money any longer. You can make the money as you go. It is not your inexperience any longer. You don't need any experience to create a remarkable new company. I didn't have any. Steve Jobs didn't have any. Bill Gates didn't have any. The Google* boys didn't have any, nor did Martha Stewart, Debbie Fields, or Ben & Jerry. Almost no one who starts a business has any experience at all. So you don't need any business experience, either.

All you need is a Dream. A Vision. A Purpose. A Mission.

All you need is a Great Idea inspired by Passion; educated by your life; trained by whatever it was that taught you whatever you know; coached by those who cared about you when you needed direction; and mentored by Love.

You've got everything you need to start, and that's where you are right now. At the start. Realize that this is not first about starting a business. No. Your business isn't the Start-up. You are the Start-up. The Start-up is You!

If you had any doubts before this, the road now is clear ahead! Come dream with me, dear reader. Because we haven't even begun this great thing yet.

■

# 21

# The Wisdom of Process

"I am not an idea man," says Dr. V. "The task is not to
aspire to some heaven but to make everyday life divine."

—Harriet Rubin, "The Perfect Vision of Dr. V,"
*Entrepreneur* magazine

Our fictitious friend John Blackwell came face-to-face with the
company *Who Is Manny Espinosa?* when he read the first
White Paper, the beginning of the Manny Espinosa Story. To begin
the development of the Mission, John reread the following White
Paper four or five times before we met to discuss it. I include it here
for your review.

## WHO IS MANNY ESPINOSA?
### *A White Paper for a Business Revolution*

#### INTRODUCTION

From coast to coast, in urban centers and suburban communities
alike, the service industry is facing a disproportionate dilemma in its
ability to hire, train, inspire, and retain an effective and loyal employee base.

The attrition rates and associated costs—in the restaurant, retail, hospitality, administrative, and production industries—are staggering. Consider the evidence, the employee attrition statistics from the U.S. Department of Labor in 2004:

■ Restaurant and hospitality industries experience a turn-over rate of 80 to 120 percent annually. Fast-food restaurants alone experienced as high as 300 percent turnover annually.
■ Retail businesses: more than 31 percent annually.
■ Administrative industry: 13 percent annually.
■ Production and manufacturing industries: as much as 25 percent annually.
■ Construction industry: more than 23 percent annually.

Employee attrition is the central problem facing these industries. From it stem the other mitigating factors that affect a company's profitability and perceived value in its community—cost of goods, payroll, health care, and so on—the average cost to train each of these employees' replacements is sometimes 100 to 200 percent of the employee's original base salary. It is estimated that the cost to replace the millions of employees who leave their jobs each year totals more than $75 billion annually.

Look at any key metric indicator and the conclusion drawn is the same: when it comes to people, the services and goods industries are broken and in need of a significant transformation. There is simply no doubt about it.

These statistics are the symptoms, pointing to a deeper issue regarding employee attrition: the perceived value of the entry-level position among American workers and the need for a revolutionary and effective new model the service industry can use to create disciplined and motivated employees for the long term.

The entry-level position is seen today as a dead-end path rather than the first step in a pursuit of limitless possibilities regarding career fulfillment, personal growth, and economic improvement. Attitudes about entry-level positions have undergone a radical transformation from even just fifty years ago, to the detriment of service-oriented businesses and the communities they serve.

Fifty years ago, entry-level service jobs were filled by a much narrower demographic of people. The people filling these jobs were the same young people delivering papers, washing cars, mowing lawns, and so on, who then discovered the means to create more discretionary income in a more efficient way.

Call them the Fifties Kids. To the Fifties Kids, the entry-level jobs in the restaurant industry were not thought of as a path to the future, but as an opportunity for the present. The Fifties Kids were focused on creating discretionary income to satisfy their current life needs and wants, rather than focused on a career opportunity. Their future then, in the fifties, and sixties, was one of hope. In a bullishly expanding economy, almost every Caucasian kid had the opportunity to dream about the American Dream . . . abundance was evident everywhere they looked. As for work, the restaurant jobs were seen for what they were, a stopover between life now and life later. The Fifties Kids were going on to college, they aspired to grow, as opposed to growing up in the restaurant job. The developmental strategies inherent to the service industry then served the demographics and needs of its employees well. The industry thrived as the new model of efficiency and service and discretionary income for many tens of thousands of young people who had a future, who were bullish about America.

Since then, as the general population in the United States has grown, so has that of our various ethnic communities, especially the Hispanic community. Totaling over 41 million people as of July 2005 (currently accounting for more than 14 percent of our total population), the Hispanic community is expected to add another 32 million people to the total U.S. population by 2025.* With greater diversification of the industry's employee pool, service-oriented businesses began to have a harder time fitting their old employee development strategies to new demographics, resulting in their current attrition problem.

## MEET MANNY ESPINOSA

Take snapshots of our inner cities and urban centers today and, all too often, they will reveal overwhelming evidence of apathy, anger, hopelessness, helplessness, and disconnect among Latino youth. For so many Latinos, the ideals associated with the American Dream are wholly unattainable and irrelevant to *their* reality.

The evidence of this disconnect is plentiful—high crime rates, lackluster school performance, and substandard health care. Entire communities are constantly living life at or below the poverty line.

Unlike the Fifties Kids, Latino youth have discovered so many ways to grow up feeling inadequate, inept, and unable to affect any real change in their lives. Indeed, few really connect with what the American Dream really represents.

Every turn in their lives encourages them to believe in nothing and *dismiss* the idea of dreaming altogether. In their environment, their examples of success are the gangster and the dealer—reminders that destructive behavior is the righteous path to power and respect.

---

* www.census.gov/population/www/projections/ppl47.html

The perpetual violence of hopelessness may have originated as an urban problem, but it has spread to affect suburban and rural communities, poor and affluent communities, diverse communities of every shape and size. The lines of how we define the inner city have blurred beyond recognition because the symptoms affect us collectively.

Meet Manny Espinosa. Manny isn't someone you or I necessarily know personally, but he or she is someone we know all the same.

We see him/her every day—flipping burgers, cleaning hotel rooms, mowing lawns, washing cars, mopping floors, digging ditches—or just waiting on corners all across America, hoping to make a few dollars this day to support himself/herself and his/her family.

Manny is the face of the seventeen- to twenty-four-year-old men and women at the center of our Latino communities, struggling to make ends meet in urban centers and smaller towns alike.

### About Manny E.

Most will agree that education is fundamentally important to the success of our youth, but Manny struggles in our school systems. The U.S. Census Bureau estimated dropout rates for Latinos ages sixteen to twenty-four in 2004 to be nearly 40 percent, despite comprising only 17 percent of the population. Nearly 14 percent of the 602,000 Latinos ages eighteen to nineteen did not finish high school in 2004, and the numbers were worse for the older youth of our target demographic: For Latinos ages twenty to twenty-one, 21.5 percent of 679,000 did not graduate. For Latinos ages twenty-two to twenty-four the rate increased to 26.6 percent of 1 million+.

Strong messaging against speaking one's native language in America is part of the conditioning infused into our educational system. We teach Manny that his/her competitive edge disappears without competent English-speaking skills, but we lack the tools to cultivate these skills with any consistency.

While the median income for the Latino population was about $34,000 in 2004, Manny is a member of the 51 percent making less than the median. He/she is often part of the 18.5 percent of the Latino community that struggles to make even half of the median income: $17,000 annually, clearly an income that is inadequate for anyone to live on, much less grow and thrive on.

Unemployment among the Latino community was roughly 6 percent in 2005, not as high as some demographic groups, but higher than average and a considerable statistic given the median income among Latino workers was 33 percent to 67 percent less than non-Latino workers. This is hardly an American Dream for Manny to write home about and call his/her own. (*U.S. Census: Income, Poverty, and Health Insurance Coverage in the United States: 2004*)

In 2005, the average duration of unemployment for the Latino worker was sixteen weeks. Of the 1.2 million Latinos recorded as unemployed in 2005, Manny is one of the 51 percent who held a job for fewer than fifteen weeks of the year. (Bureau of Labor Statistics)

Manny lacks access to the most basic of health care for himself and his family. In 2004, the Census Bureau reported that more than 30 percent of the Hispanic population was uninsured, a rate 40 percent higher than the next ethnic group.

In summary, Manny is poor, uneducated, barely employable, and while dissatisfied with his/her status in society, is too beaten down every day to challenge it. He/she is the stereotype, the pariah, the face of those whose potential we most take for granted. He/she is at the bottom of the service industry's food chain, and will always be there because we expect so little from Manny and give less in return.

But, perhaps more important, Manny expects so little from himself/herself.

## AN INDUSTRY HUNGRY FOR NEW SOLUTIONS

The service industry clearly sees the people of the Latino community as an important resource upon which to build the growth of their businesses. The problem they face is in how to train and develop world-class employees in a way that is also cost efficient for the business. This presents a significant challenge. The same people from the Latino community on whom the businesses' profitability is relying are also people who have had few examples of real success, and little or no training in how to get there.

Employers' recruiting, hiring, and development options have become severely skewed and limited. The number of those who are barely employable among Latinos increases, as does the employer's reality to settle for less, to settle for barely employable just to put bodies in their business and keep operations treading water.

Few companies acknowledge the price they're paying for accepting this status quo of employee attrition: employees conditioned to expect less of themselves, achieve less, and subsequently contribute less to the company's bottom line and sustainability. All of which feeds back into how the company relates to the community.

We've created a perpetuating cycle of mediocrity driven from both sides by messages of hopelessness, helplessness, and ineffectual behavior. The service industry is invested in their communities and hungry for new solutions. All it takes is for someone with a bold new perspective to help both employer and employee experience a paradigm shift.

The so-called training initiatives and systems that the service industry invents do too little to fix the problem. Even if a company's intention is to cultivate excellence in the individual, the Latino community isn't listening. Despite the businesses' intentions, the reality that actually shows up for so many Latinos every day is one where gangs, violence, and excess poverty are the example, a reality in which the entry-level position is not typically seen as a way out of their downward spiral.

The message of the American Dream has worn thin because its symbolism and the pain of Latinos' actual experience are often a mismatch. If many Latinos are performing poorly in school, lack discipline, lack command of English language skills, have few examples of success in their communities, have only low-level jobs available to them, or a combination of all of these factors, one can easily understand how some in the Latino community might feel defeated even before they get started, and the frustration that the service industry feels in turn.

A more holistic approach to training and development certainly makes sense—using the entry-level position to develop the *whole* person. Realistically, it's an investment *not* made in poor communities because the employer has no real idea how to do it.

Think about it—if we've settled for creating a culture of mediocrity for these souls, and the cost of training them effectively is not cost effective due to the high likelihood of turnover, what is the motivation for making the investment in the first place? There is none. What is needed is a new model that develops the people with the least amount of hope into employees that come smarter, develop faster, cost less, and produce more than any others that the service industry has seen.

## SOLVING THE EMPLOYEE ATTRITION PROBLEM

The services and goods industries are broken and in need of a significant transformation of attitude that says that making just enough of a contribution is good enough to one where companies are consistently creating world-class employees at every level of their organization. We've wallowed for long enough in a status quo where 100 percent attrition is a reasonable expectation, where expecting 100 percent turnover matches the life reality of our struggling communities.

What if there were a business model for your industry that:

- Reduces employee attrition rates by 40 percent, 50 percent, or more?
- Creates a shift in how a community perceives the contribution its restaurants, hotels, developers, and manufacturing plants make to the community?
- Creates a change in attitude within a community about its businesses' ability to cultivate excellence in its citizens?
- Is responsible for reconnecting families and communities through newly discovered wellsprings of discipline and integrity among its youth?
- Is the catalyst for the children of our urban communities to achieve new levels of academic and professional excellence, beyond the scope of the service industry?
- Redefines how we recruit and develop and reestablish the value of the entry-level position?
- Rebuilds the American workforce by infusing into its culture the importance of starting where you are, mastering the skills you need to get to the next level, and seeing every aspect of one's life as an opportunity to practice and grow?

- ■ Is an active and integral part of the developmental solution our economy is looking for?
- ■ Produces a high ROI while being able to uncover and heal some of the root problems of the "barely employable" in America?

We ask these types of questions all the time, and we hear the same answers all the time: "That would be great but . . . we can't get employees who work hard enough, who want to grow . . . we can't pay them what they want to be paid . . . can't get a quality employee for what we can pay . . . can't get our employees to care about doing their job right . . . they're just going to turn around and quit soon anyway."

So we ask a simple question: "What if you could?" And the answer is usually silence because the industry simply lacks the means to develop the barely employable at a cost the service-oriented business can justify.

In spite of the conditioned responses, we have discovered the business model that will break that deafening silence by producing a entirely new class of entry-level employees from every ethnic community including Latinos, helping to provide the service industry with the best employees they've ever hired—period.

## *WHO IS MANNY ESPINOSA?* IS THE SOLUTION

*Who Is Manny Espinosa?* is a brilliant new scalable franchise business model, conceived, and dreamed by Michael Gerber, founder of E-Myth Worldwide and its highly successful collective of small business tools. It is a business model that will revolutionize the relationship between the American worker and the entry-level position.

It thrives on a *think—believe—feel—produce* paradigm shift that says that there are no victims on either side of the attrition struggle, that everyone can win if they are simply shown how in an effective manner. There are nonprofit and governmental agencies dedicated to this pursuit, but no business has taken up the challenge to revolutionize recruitment and development strategies the way that *Who Is Manny Espinosa?* will, answering the most important questions the investor and the industry have to ask:

- Can you do it?
- Can you do it cost effectively?
- Can you make money?

The answer to all three questions is a resounding *yes*.

At the heart of *Who Is Manny Espinosa?* is a recruitment and staffing agency for the restaurant, hospitality, retail, construction, and production industries. However, unlike traditional recruiting or staffing agencies, *Who Is Manny Espinosa?*, the Company, integrates a comprehensive training and development component designed to redefine how the so-called barely employable *value* the nature of the service and goods industries *and* the nature of their own potential. Combined, *Who Is Manny Espinosa?* will be a recruitment and development firm unlike any the workplace has seen.

## THE MODEL

We consider *Who Is Manny Espinosa?* to be a Life Academy: a continuing intense experience that demands high participation, commitment, and accountability from its students, but offers even greater benefits to the student, industry, and community in the long term. It is a transformative, sustainable lifelong experience that instills vision in its participants along with a belief system that there is a better life available to each of us. We only have to make a declaration to achieve it, and align our actions in a way that propels us forward on the right path.

As a Life Academy, *Who Is Manny Espinosa?*'s primary purpose is to create world-class employees for entry-level positions in the service industry while shaping them into world-class Independents, as opposed to dependents, people who are focused on personal growth and financial independence. Students will be taught how developing unbridled enthusiasm for the art of learning and practice is relevant to achieving their dreams, starting as an apprentice at every level of their development and achieving mastery before moving on.

Enrollees in a Manny E. recruitment and development firm sign a life contract that includes full participation in the whole student development plan *and* a commitment to practice while giving back to their community of family, peers, friends, and the communities in which they live. The structure of the development program is built on the idea that practicing the right skills leads to superior results. Students will initially commit to a rigorous six-week training program, the make-or-break opportunity for each to get on board. One hundred percent participation and accountability will be demanded in exchange for this life-changing experience, beginning with the following skill sets:

## Street Skills

The first set of curriculum develops the student's relationship with the world. These skills are most rudimentary for a Manny E. recruit to master:

- **Knowledge of the world and what it wants.** What is true about the world and what does Manny need to develop personally and professionally in order to participate in it effectively? Manny needs to learn that what is demanded of him/her includes commitment, discipline, the willingness to practice, and the ability to speak English sufficiently so that he/she can understand others and be understood, to be able to relate to a wide range of people. The world needs Manny to be able to look at the business community and identify how it defines successful performance.

- **Knowledge of yourself and what you need to know.** If Manny takes an inventory of the knowledge and skills he/she needs to have to maximize potential, what will he/she discover? Manny needs to learn more about interpersonal communication and the art of listening. He/she needs to learn what it is to grow into a leadership role, to be dedicated to learning, and to understand that development requires the patience and faith necessary to achieve success one step at a time. He/she needs to learn to value impeccability and punctuality—the value of showing up.

- **Knowledge of results and what you need to know to produce them.** Manny must deepen his/her self-inventory and create a relationship with who he/she *is* and what the world expects of him/her. Manny needs to know how the business operates, how it defines productivity. He/she needs to know the technical skills required for the position they're filling. Manny needs to know about profitability and the financial side of business. He/she needs to learn how to internalize this new model for success and spread it back into his/her community, creating a more global paradigm shift. Manny needs to learn how to manage conflict in order to be able to operate effectively within an organizational structure.

- **Knowledge of what's next and how to improve upon excellence and move on.** The process of developing oneself is creative and cyclical, requiring constant reflection and determining how to do something better, more efficiently, more impeccably, and so on, the next time. Manny needs to learn how to set long-term goals, identify the steps required to achieve them, and plan his/her actions for success. He/she needs to learn how to look at any breakdown critically, stay open to possibilities, and invent new solutions.

### Life Skills

At the same time the Manny E. recruit develops his or her mastery of these Street Skills, he or she will begin the study and practice of Life Skills. These skills will redefine the role of the entry-level job in helping the student get from point A to point B, from here to fulfillment:

- **Concentration.** In a world that is constantly accelerating, so many find it harder and harder to stay present and stay focused. As a result, we often do not achieve the level of mastery of our lives that we should. Instead of practicing the art of being where we are, we spend much of our days trapped in either past memory or future imagination, both of which we allow to create an inaccurate picture of our present. In Manny's case, there is little more than struggle and hopelessness to be found in his/her past memory, so the present he/she experiences and the future he/she imagines is just as bleak. By teaching Manny that in the present moment lie unlimited possibilities and that living in that space is practice, we help him/her begin a paradigm shift.

- **Discrimination.** Discrimination is the practice of focusing on those things that are most important, on choices that will deliver the best results as efficiently as possible. For Manny, in an entry-level position, the focus will likely need to be on mastering only the skills that will lead him/her to the next level of development. It will be holding in mind the truth that an entry-level position can be more than just a dead-end job. It can be the first of many steps each of us take to live a more successful and fulfilled life. If Manny needs to first learn how to focus on the living, present moment that holds the most possibilities, then he/she next needs to focus in that moment on the actions that will deliver the greatest long-term reward.

- **Organization.** Mastering the skills of concentration and discrimination takes energy and effort. More important, they require the space to allow one's intentions and actions to align properly. This skill teaches Manny how best to organize his/her life to achieve immediate and long-lasting results. This is organization of his home, his workplace, his actions, his behavior, his intentions, every aspect of his life. Organization is about creating order out of chaos. Manny's world of being barely employable is chaos. What Manny will learn is the alchemy of his life that is necessary to get results.

- **Innovation.** Focus on the present and its possibilities, on the behaviors and actions that are most important, in an organized environment, allow for teaching of the fourth Life Skill, how to be innovative. Innovation is the belief that there is a way to do everything and, if that is so, there is a better and best way to do everything. Innovation is a commitment to incremental and continuous improvement, a belief system that Manny must have in order to see how this entry-level step is going to lead to greater accomplishments, and that by seeing the possibilities of improving his/her condition, he/she can begin to see how to reinvent them, to create new ways of working in the world, of defining his/her reality, of transforming his/her life.

▪ **Communication.** This skill is essential for any of us to master if we are to achieve the results and the outcome we deserve. It is one thing to be focused, organized, and innovative. But for any dream to become a reality, we require the help of other people. At a Manny E. center, we will teach the student how to master the art of effective communication and negotiation, and provide him/her with the support network needed for long-term success.

## Work Skills

The pot of gold at the end of the six-week intensive will be placement in an entry-level, service-industry position. Manny E. regards all entry-level positions not as jobs, but as school. An entry-level position for all Manny E. students is a paid education. Because it is a paid education as opposed to a job, the student sees that job in a completely different light. He is being paid to learn, and, as he does well in school he is being prepared to graduate to the next level where he gets paid even more for his achievement. In short, by the time these six weeks are over, we will have transformed Manny into a world-class apprentice. Fifty years ago, it was common knowledge that everyone started from the beginning somewhere in the work world, and that with the right effort and enthusiasm applied to the mastery of skills, the sky was the limit. The launch of *Who Is Manny Espinosa?* marks a return to those ideals, updated to include the whole fabric of our communities.

The Street Skills and Life Skills with which each Manny E. graduate enters the work force create a solid foundation for the work-specific skills his/her employer will layer onto the development process. And, the employer will come to equate a Manny E. graduate with a completely different attitude that defines commitment and excellence.

The end of the six-week intensive does not spell the end of the Manny E. R&D firm's contributions to the graduate's development. Remember that the fifth Life Skill is the ability to rely on other people to help them to achieve their goals. Manny E. graduates will continue their development by attending a three-hour seminar once per week at Manny E. Academy. In addition, an online Manny E. community will be created to enable Manny E. centers to provide graduates with long-term coaching and mentoring. Monthly curriculum, combined with peer mentoring, will be assigned to Manny E. graduates, which will supplement their development.

Finally, every graduate of the six-week intensive will be assigned to a Manny E. Group of seven graduates, led by a Manny E. Facilitator to share experiences, learning difficulties, work-related frustrations and successes, as each member grows to be more successful by assimilating the tools, training, and development coaching they are provided on a week-to-week basis.

## A PROGRESSIVE EXPERIENCE

Registering and enrolling at a *Who Is Manny Espinosa?* recruitment and development center will be a *progressive* experience for its students. Completion of the core curriculum not only empowers them to be exceptional at an entry-level position, but also grooms them to become the internal bench candidates that every service-oriented business depends on.

It is much more cost effective for an organization to promote from within rather than expend additional resources on training new candidates. Instead, employees use the core skills learned as a foundation upon which to build incremental and lasting development at a whole new level.

Advanced training and development at a Manny E. center will include a comprehensive education about the skill and art of managing people, and of managing all aspects of businesses' operations. In teaching Manny how to master the skills to get to the next level, the one beyond that, and so on, we are setting him/her up to take on and master the skills needed to become a world-class manager in the service and goods industries.

Graduates of Manny Espinosa R&D centers will be able to reciprocate what they've learned to future generations of students, serving as recruiters, teachers, managers, community development leaders, and support staff at *Who Is Manny Espinosa?* centers nationwide.

## AN INTEGRATED EXPERIENCE

The curriculum at every Manny E. recruitment and development firm will be taught by individuals with expertise in wide-ranging fields. This high-energy, high-intensity transformative experience will rely on the contributions of athletes, business executives, personal development coaches, martial arts instructors, and so on.

We are committed to working *with* Manny E. students—with the most forgotten members of our communities—from the ground up, to instill discipline, focus, self-respect, community activism, and a commitment to the practice of excellence. What employers will get from a Manny E. graduate is an individual who transcends what the employer has been conditioned to expect—they will get an individual who is a partner in transforming the industry. What Manny E. students will get is the support of a company that is involved in their development, that collaborates with our "barely employable" youth to help move them up the ladder, one rung at a time.

## IMMEDIATE RETURN ON INVESTMENT

As a scalable, replicable franchise model, *Who Is Manny Espinosa?* is a concept that is primed to be the most effective turnkey solution among its peers. Much as Manpower or any other employment firm is paid by employers to find and supply recruits, so will be the case with *Who Is Manny Espinosa?* The difference will be in the quality of the recruits and how quickly and effectively they are able to transform an employer's relationship with its customer. Employers will associate the Manny E. brand with being the solution, synonymous with results and transformative experience, and look to a Manny E. firm *first* for their staffing needs.

*Who Is Manny Espinosa?* sees its primary customers as:

- Food services, hospitality, administrative, retail, and construction industries.
- Federal, state, and local employment development agencies, for whom we can both be the model of effectiveness.
- High schools, community organizations, and parents in need of fresh, new solutions for lifting our "barely employable" youth out of limiting belief systems, pointing the next generation to a bold new path of effectiveness and empowerment.

As a scalable franchise model, *Who Is Manny Espinosa?* creates a perfect opportunity for ownership by the communities that we serve. The U.S. Census estimates the Latino community will account for nearly half the American population by the year 2050. This has already created a huge amount of ethnic purchasing power among our Latino brothers and sisters, the effect of which will only increase with predicted population trends. Companies are increasingly marketing to Latinos and other ethnic groups. Additionally, the number of Latino-owned businesses is on the rise, numbering nearly 1.6 million with annual sales of $222 billion in 2002. *Who Is Manny Espinosa?* primes itself to be an investment opportunity that feeds the community—its economics and spirit.

*Who Is Manny Espinosa?* R&D firms will become known as the proprietary leader in its recruitment and development field, always operating under the mantra "World Class People Yield World Class Results." The question is, who will join us to steward the vision to its potential?

■

John Blackwell and I met shortly after he had read the Manny E. White Paper. He had a manila folder on his desk, squarely settled at right angles to where he sat in his desk chair. I sat down across from him. There was no small talk. John started the conversation off immediately. It was one week to the day since he had become COO of *Who Is Manny Espinosa?*

John began. "Hello, Michael. Thanks for making the time to join me here. I know you'll find our meeting a valuable expenditure of your time. I have made the first pass at creating a Mission, and the accompanying Strategy and Plan we'll need for accomplishing it. I could just as easily have sent it to you, but I thought we could get a lot more done this way. Should you have any questions, I can immediately answer them. So, let's get started. You won't need to read your copy. I'll talk you through it, and then you can review it at your leisure. If you'll turn it over, it immediately becomes a notepad you can use while we discuss my thoughts, Strategy, and Plan. Okay?"

I turned the sheaf of paper over, and just as John had indicated, each page was headed by the words: "Manny Espinosa Strategy & Plan NOTES."

"Wonderful," I said. "Let's get started.

# STOP
### AND
# FOCUS

## The Wisdom of Process

*Trust me on this: The wisdom of the process is to begin it.*

*What does that mean? It means that until you actually take the first step, you can't take the second, and until you take the second step, you can't take the third, and the result you are here to produce will only reveal itself to you until, and after, you have committed yourself to the Path. The Path of Impossibilities. The Path of the Outrageous. The Path that everyone will tell you isn't real, is just a figment of your imagination.*

*Isn't that a remarkable expression: "a figment of your imagination"? It presumes that your imagination makes up things that aren't real, as though that is the opposite of things that are real, the kinds of things that have nothing to do with your imagination.*

*All the left-brained behemoths in the world would have you believe that imagination is the problem, when, in fact, the entire universe is supremely imaginative. Whether or not you believe in God, who can fail to be amazed at the incredible world in which we live?*

*How deadening would it be if we extricated our imagination from our lives? What would this world be without our positive imagination, our starstruck imagination, our joyful, playful, exotic, mystical, spiritual imagination? Where would art be, or music, or literature, or philosophy, or religion, or works of the* spirit, or architecture, or love, or solidarity, or humanity, or parenting, or caring for our parents when they cannot care for themselves?

Imagination is what happens when a grand, great, all-consuming idea possesses us like the one that possessed Martin Luther King, to cause him to blurt out with all the passion a human being can muster, "I have a dream!"

What does that mean in the day-to-day reality of things? We take that first fateful step, and then the second—and, yes, I am here, walking alongside you—now the third and the fourth and we're on our way! Look what just happened! Isn't this amazing that we're actually doing what we only dreamed about doing a short while ago?

# 22

# Beginning the Strategy; Beginning the Plan

Often an idea would occur to me which seemed to have
force . . . I never let one of those ideas escape me, but
wrote it on a scrap of paper and put it in that drawer. In
that way I saved my thoughts on the subject, and, you
know, such things often come in a kind of intuitive way
more clearly than if one were to sit down and deliberately
reason them out. To save the results of such mental action
is true intellectual economy . . . Of course, in this
instance, I had to arrange the material at hand and
adapt it to the particular case presented.

—Abraham Lincoln

Usually, at the beginning of a relationship, there is a great deal
of fussing and musing and getting situated. A new manager
needs to find his place, get connected to the people he's going to work
with, move into his new office and put the things he always takes
with him away, on the wall, on the top of the desk, and in the filing
cabinets.

At the beginning there's usually a pause, a reconsideration, a
thoughtful few weeks to settle into the fact of a new job, a new ac-

countability, a new future that has to be organized in such a way as to make the new resident in it feel comfortable.

There was none of that with John Blackwell. He simply moved in, threw his bag in the corner, and started the process without delay.

He smiled, opened his sheaf of papers, looked at me briefly as though to say, "Ready?" and started his presentation.

"The importance of this project has finally become clear to me, Michael. I knew it was big, but I never truly took in the immensity of it. I also never truly took in the simplicity of it. This is not only doable, it is eminently doable. That's part of what excites me so. Taking the model apart, and putting it together as a very small business at the beginning is how we're going to design the finished product, build it, and get it ready to roll out. My belief is that we can accomplish all of it in less than two years. At least that's what I am planning to do. Within eighteen months of your approval of my Strategy & Plan, *Manny Espinosa,* the Company, will have prepared itself to grow exponentially by year two.

"So, let me describe my Strategy and then my Plan, and you tell me what I've left out, if anything.

"My Strategy is to build a *Manny Espinosa* practice, as you call it, right here in San Diego. We will sell it as a work in process to two or three major restaurant systems, to have them participate with us as Strategic Partners in a test. Our role is to produce a continuing stream of candidates to them for a fixed dollar amount, yet to be determined, and to work with them to make certain that they and their people are ready to absorb each candidate into their system in a select number of outlets as part of a personnel development program they are testing. There is no need for anyone in their organization to know any more about it than that.

"The 'how' of it naturally will be worked out by me with their management teams long in advance of the first candidates we send them. So, that part of my Strategy calls for a ready channel waiting for each candidate as soon as he graduates from our Six-Week Intensive. That is the first step of the Strategy: a ready and receptive market for our product. Given the circumstances of attrition in the restaurant industry, that will be easy to accomplish. In fact, I have already begun to make appointments with top-level executives in three restaurant systems: Taco Bell, McDonald's, and Quiznos. If these three don't respond quickly enough and enthusiastically enough, we'll then go on to my next three choices, and my third three, and my fourth. But, whoever our strategic partners end up being, there will be three, and they will be participating within the time frame I have committed to you.

"The second part of my Strategy is to identify, contact, and begin a conversation with no more than ten program developers to join us in building the first Six-Week in time for a launch six months from now. That launch date is critical if we're going to meet our eighteen-month objective. We have to get each 'Manny' trained and onto the floor of his employer's restaurant if we're going to get the experience we need to immediately improve upon our beta Six-Week. This will obviously need to happen several times before Launch Date Two happens twenty-four months from now. So, Step Two of our strategy is to build the personal-development system to begin the transformation of our young candidates in real time.

"The third part of my Strategy is, obviously, Manny himself. We have to create and launch a *Manny Espinosa* seminar that brings large numbers of young Latinos to a room where we can sell them our idea. This is obviously as critical to the success of our Strategy as the other two parts are. If we fail to attract, inspire, and enroll enough people to make this possible, everything else will have been for naught. And this is key to me: we can get as many people as we want into a room if we get the government and the department of employment involved; they'll simply send kids to us. We have to find the way to get large numbers of these kids to buy into our Story. Our Story, and our ability to tell it, is critical if our business idea is going to take root in the Latino/Hispanic community as it needs to if it's going to be successful.

"Finally, Stage Four of my Strategy is to seek out, identify, and enroll three Key people to serve as our Cadre, the Sergeants who are going to deliver our intensive to their *Manny* recruits. These people are obviously critical to the success of our Program. They are the ones who are going to lead, challenge, train, and mentor our graduates to make the shift from their current way of being to the one we intend for them.

"I have already made a list of twenty men and women I have known in the past that I would stake my life on. I intend to start talking to them immediately. These people will then begin the process of developing the kind of systems we need in order to make certain that Manny, the graduate, who is about to go through the worst part of his development, on the floor of a restaurant, doesn't simply get lost. This is the part where we could lose him. And my Cadre needs to make certain we don't.

"So, to repeat, the Strategy is to build our beta franchise prototype ready for launch within two years. To sign up three Strategic Restaurant Partners to help us build our system. To sign up ten program developers to build the program you describe in your White Paper. To have that program done in six months. To create and launch a *Manny Espinosa* seminar through which to enroll our first class of candidates for graduation no later than seven and a half months from now. Impossible sounding, I know, but critical if we're going to be ready to roll out our program in six months. I will write the seminar and deliver the seminar myself. I've already started, and have gotten some help from several kick-ass Latino friends of mine who were only too willing to help me. The final part of the Strategy is to recruit no fewer than three Cadre members—my Sergeants—who know how to engage young people in a process of change. They will be dedicated, strong, committed, and have the kind of bearing we need. They will be incredible models of discipline, training, excellence, and compassion.

"My Plan, Michael, is to set up an Action Plan on the whiteboard behind me, listing all the benchmarks that must be met, along with the budget, the accountability, and the due dates for everything to keep on target.

"To do all this, I'll need a limited staff of one full-time executive assistant, one financial modeler part time, and one doofus who will do whatever I need him to do to make certain my back is always covered as I'm rocking and rolling to get things done.

"As for pay, I have already picked my executive assistant, and she's already agreed to work for minimum wage for the first three months provided that when we achieve the result I'm committed to achieve by then, she gets a raise to thirty-six thousand dollars. She knows this is a spare process, but she is so in love with the idea that she was willing to come to work for free if I needed her to. The financial modeler will cost us twenty dollars per hour for three hours a day three times a week. That's all I'll really need from him. He's a full-time graduate student, and he's ready to start once you say yes. Again, he loves the Dream and wants to be a part of it. The doofus is another story. He's my son. Lives at home. He's an extraordinary guy who simply said, 'Yes,' and doesn't need any assurances of any kind. He also loves the Dream, buys into the Story, and told me that if I didn't include him he'd move out of the house. I told him that I couldn't pay him any more than minimum wage at the beginning, and he laughed and reminded me that I haven't paid him any more than minimum wage for as long as I've known him, so why should this be any different?

"As for the program developers, I can get them involved for some kind of a royalty once the program is up and running. I haven't begun those conversations yet, but I have great confidence in my ability to do that.

"Finally, there's the Cadre. I can convince them to do this without pay for the first six months. A number of them are retired military. Some might need a salary to start. Once I begin my conversations with them, I'll know more about what we're talking about. But for now, I believe it will be no more than thirty-five thousand dollars a year. On the other hand, I've begun to noodle with a royalty-based system where they get paid based on the number of kids they put through each Intensive. In any case, I've put my expectations into a financial model for you to review.

"Whatever we decide about costs, my intention is to get our Strategic Partners to pick up the cost for us, plus make us a little profit as we build the program. To them, this will be chump change. All we need to do is show them the wisdom of our deliverable and get them to see it as an investment in change, but mostly an investment in improvement. The real truth is, I expect no later than a year from now that these Strategic Restaurant Partners and many more like them will become key investors in *Who Is Manny Espinosa?* As it succeeds, they will want to participate in it.

"So, what do you think?" John Blackwell asked.

"Do it," I said.

# STOP AND FOCUS

## Beginning the Strategy; Beginning the Plan

*At the beginning of the Mission we must calculate the end. In John Blackwell's Strategy, the end was calculated to be the completed beta prototype for only six weeks, until the company was ready for rollout. Why did he consider that to be an ample test? Why did he calculate his needs to be so few? Why did he believe he could get people to participate in his Mission for so little financial remuneration, especially in these days of skyrocketing payrolls and options and all manner of benefits?*

*Go back to the standards I created for John Blackwell. See how he took them seriously. Without any further conversation about it, his Strategy and his Plan were mirrors of the standards I gave him at the outset.*

*You and your leader must honor the agreements you make with each other. If John Blackwell had come back to me with a Strategy and Plan that were completely inconsistent with the standards we had agreed upon, what do you think I would have said? What would you have said to a Leader who had provided you with a Strategy and Plan that were completely inconsistent with the rules of the game as you had spelled them out?*

*(continued)*

*What did I say to John? I said, "Do it." Period. What was there to talk about? The budget was leaner than lean, and the company would probably prove to be profitable, even in the developmental stage, if John could produce the results he was committing to.*

*The best part of it all is that he not only didn't ask for more than he believed he needed, but less. And, at the same time, he put himself on the line for the majority of the key results; creating and performing the recruitment seminar; pitching and closing the restaurant management; finding and hiring the ten developers to produce the Manny E. Intensive; finding and hiring the three Cadre he needed to deliver the programs and take accountability for Manny's success; finding, hiring, and managing the three key helpers he needed at the outset at remarkably low cost; and a Plan to pull it all off.*

*Of course, I said, "Do it!" Now I'd get to watch . . . to see what he did.*

■

# 23

## The Mission Is Under Way

*Chance furnishes me with what I need. I am like a man
who stumbles along; my foot strikes something, I bend
over and it is exactly what I want.*

—James Joyce

"This Mission *is* under way."

John Blackwell stood in front of a small group of people I
had never met—ten men and four women. I had been invited by John
to sit in on this kickoff meeting, the product of many prior meetings
he had conducted with restaurant executives and managers, hotel and
construction industry leaders, program developers, Cadre prospects,
local banks and associations, leaders of the local Latino community,
leaders of the cities in San Diego County, and Angel Investors.

This was the first time all of the players had met under one roof.
It was the first time most of them had met one another. Needless to
say, John had been busy.

Before the meeting, he spoke to me about the reception he had
received.

"Michael, I have never received such unanimous accolades about
anything I have ever been involved in. People love *Who Is Manny*

*Espinosa Project.* They immediately get it. Despite the continuous flow of questions about how it's going to work, no one doubts it *will* work. And because of that, it has been easy to get the commitments I need to keep my commitment to you. The restaurant chains are in. McDonald's, Taco Bell, and Quiznos, to name just a few. I've provided you with a complete list of the restaurant systems who want in. As for the developers, I've gotten some remarkable people to say yes. I've also included their names and their résumés for your review. They include martial artists, athletes, military leaders, teachers, trainers, business leaders, and curriculum developers. All of them are stars in their discipline of choice. If anyone can invent the System you have outlined in your white paper, these folks will. They are committed to it, and will work together to get it done on time.

"Now it's your turn," he said. "I want to introduce you to the group to reaffirm what I have already told them, in your own inimitable fashion."

As we walked into the meeting room, John motioned for me to accompany him to the front. He then turned to the group and said, "Ladies and gentlemen, we're all here for the very same reason, to transform the lives of young Hispanics and Latinos so that they can grow to their full potential. The contribution these young people can make to their families, their communities, their employers, and their peers has never been realized on the scale we anticipate in this room. I would like to introduce you to Michael Gerber, who is the visionary behind *Who Is Manny Espinosa?* Michael is the founder, CEO, and Chief Dreamer of the Company, the world's first recruitment and development firm. Michael?"

I looked at the small group of people in front of me. In my role as speaker, I have stood before thousands of groups, large and small. But this group was different. Perhaps it was the purpose that had brought us together, but there was intensity in their faces, a focus, a maturity about them that touched me immediately. This was not just an audience. This was a team on a mission! John Blackwell had done his job well, I thought. It's now my job.

"Good morning, ladies and gentlemen," I began. "I am honored to be with you today to share my thoughts and feelings about the mission we're engaged in, the mission we call *Who Is Manny Espinosa?*

"The simple fact is that life isn't fun for many billions of people on our earth. Quite far from it. Billions of people on this earth live lives of quiet—and not so quiet—desperation. First, of course, this desperation is economic. Most people in the world haven't developed what I have come to call economic ability, the ability to financially care for themselves, let alone others who depend on them. A lack of economic ability is a painful reality to so many Manny Espinosas in our world.

"That is not your problem, of course. But I propose it is your opportunity. I also am proposing that you don't possess the power to transform that reality. Only Manny Espinosa does. Our job is to identify that power, localize it, and transform it into action."

I began to tell the Story as passionately as you could imagine. I explained many, if not most, of the things I've told you in the preceding pages.

I told them about Manny's lack of rudimentary skills . . . about the glaring absence of role models in his life.

I told them that Manny doesn't think of himself as someone who matters. He wants to matter and is angry that his future is probably going to look much like his past, unless he's lucky, that is.

I told them that, for Manny, seemingly the only choice left is the gangster's life, which, while risky, at least empowers him to be Manny

Espinosa without any fear that he'll look stupid and live a life of indignity and lack of respect doing stupid work for stupid pay in the hope that years away he'll get to be a manager in a fast-food restaurant.

I told them that Manny Espinosa will only be reached if we instill in him or her a greater Dream . . . a greater Hope.

I continued. "The Company called *Who Is Manny Espinosa?* is destined to become the place where this can happen. It cannot be that place where Manny is acculturated into a straight world to become a straight citizen. It cannot be the place where we sell the American Dream. It cannot be the place where we tell Manny what everyone in the straight world is telling him: learn the language, get a good job, and save your money while you go to school. It cannot be, because if it is, it will be a disaster.

"To be successful, Manny needs to hear a different message, a contrarian's message, a message in opposition to the one he has been hearing from his parents, his teachers, the principal at his school. Manny isn't stupid. He looks at them and says to himself, 'Right. And what has that gotten you?' No, the Mannys of the world need leaders, teachers, tutors, trainers, and Cadre who symbolize a life that has never been his or her experience. A strange, new, exciting, exhilarating life. A life worth living. Where Manny is physically, emotionally, spiritually, and mentally a Hero. A member of the Hero Class. A Leader. That's what you and I are here to do, ladies and gentlemen. That's the job ahead of us. That is what it is going to take for Manny Espinosa to take his place, his Hero's place, in this world we live in.

"Thank you for participating in Manny's quest. Any questions you have are welcome."

I stopped, took a deep breath, and waited for what would happen next.

■

A man at the back of the room raised his hand. He was dressed in a pair of gray slacks and a casual striped shirt, with a logo I couldn't quite make out embroidered above the breast pocket.

"Yes, sir," I said, motioning to him. "Your name?"

"Mr. Gerber, I'm Jerry Long from McDonald's. Let me be straight with you. The last thing we would want is for Manny to think he is better than a manager at McDonald's. If this program is going to work, that's what we would *hope* he will be. If he *isn't* going to become a manager at McDonald's, in fact, doesn't even *want* to be, why in the world would we hire him?"

"Great question, Jerry. And here's the answer. You would hire Manny because you will have the best shot you have ever had at encouraging a crew worker to want to become a manager at McDonald's. And that's because Manny is motivated. He sees McDonald's as a *school*, not as a *job*. Your store is a school where he gets to practice the skills you and we are teaching him, the skills that are called for if he is going to succeed in ways he never imagined. Manny is there to learn the skills of concentration, discrimination, organization, innovation, and communication. He knows if he doesn't learn, it's his fault, not yours. So, first of all, you get someone who has been prepped for you, like no entry-level person you've ever hired. He's ready.

"Second, Manny is a blank piece of paper for your company, except for this: we have told him a story about life at *Who Is Manny Espinosa?* We've told him that most of us—yes, you and me, too, Jerry—aren't clear about who we are and what we want to do. Most of us are living stories that other people have made up for us.

"But to be a Hero, we need to create our own Stories built upon the truth. What is our purpose here? What are we destined to do? How does our perception of reality shape reality? What does it mean to be a human being here on this earth? What causes us to learn, to grow, to be challenged, and to rise to that challenge?

"For Manny, life is a very big and exciting question, not a dismal, limiting, and dreary answer. It's not about a job. It's about a calling, just like it was for the founder of your company, Ray Kroc. We're telling Manny that becoming an entrepreneur in this age of the new entrepreneur is his true opportunity to become a true Hero. It's not about getting a job, but about creating jobs for many, many people.

"Where would he best learn how to do that? At McDonald's, of course. Or at Taco Bell, or Quiznos, or in any one of thousands of places created by entrepreneurs. What a great opportunity for the company that hires him at the very beginning. He couldn't be more perfect for you!"

Jerry from McDonald's obviously wasn't satisfied with my answer. "So, what happens when this kid comes to work and tells everyone else on the job what he's doing? He immediately becomes special, and everyone else on the job becomes distracted by his story. Do you see the problem this will create for the manager of that operation?"

"Yes, I do," I responded. "But what I also see is that this is your chance to talk about the *Manny Espinosa Project* with all of your employees. You can tell them that McDonald's, in its forward-thinking way, is determined to revolutionize the lives of its employees and its company. *Manny Espinosa*, the Company, is just one way you are doing this. And, yes, it's a challenge. Anything new is. But Manny Espinosa is at the cutting edge of people development for your entire industry, Jerry. Besides, what's the worst thing that could happen? Your annual attrition rate is already at 300 percent! Do you think Manny is going to make it any worse?"

A second hand went up.

"My name is Walter Hensley. I teach martial arts, and I was told my skills would be important for this project. Can you tell me why?"

"Yes, Walter, I can. The training we're going to be putting Manny through has never been done before. I think of it as organic training, because it deals with the whole of the person, not just individual parts. We're not training Manny to do a job. This is not a vocational school. We are preparing Manny for life. You are all here to work as a team to integrate your disciplines into a holistic training that will transform the way Manny thinks about himself and the world. Martial arts will provide one key to the door. But until all of the keys are turned, the door won't open. The door is Manny's freedom, his path to liberation. None of you have done this before, I know. But that's what's so exciting about it. You get to do what everyone else would call the impossible."

More hands went up. I motioned to a woman who had a dubious expression on her face.

"Mr. Gerber, my name is Alicia Huntley. I am a language instructor. My concern is, how do you expect Manny to learn to speak English fluently enough to excel on the job, while also learning all these other skills? I think if Manny just learns English, he'll be well ahead of the game as far as his employer is concerned."

"Yes, that may be true. But we're not interested in helping Manny get 'well ahead of the game,' as you put it. We want Manny to play a completely different game than one would expect of him. It's the Hero's Game. And learning how to speak English has nothing whatsoever to do with being a Hero. Learning English is simply a way for Manny to express his power.

"That's what is so important to understand about this Project. We are building *A Course for Heroes*. We're not training Manny how to *do*. We're training Manny how to *be*. And none of us knows how to do that. But . . . and this is what I'm counting on . . . we all know *something* about it. One of you knows about martial arts. One of you knows about discipline. One of you knows about learning. One of you knows about meditation. In short, all of you know what Manny needs to know to become a Hero. Your job is to give it to him."

John Blackwell walked to the front of the room, thanked me for my time, and said, "Okay, everyone, let's take a break and reconvene in ten minutes."

# STOP AND FOCUS

## The Mission Is Under Way

*The Mission is under way!*

*As I spoke to the group of developers, the true essence of the Manny Espinosa Project revealed itself! It was to become, and be known as, A Course for Heroes®.*

*Before I said that, it did not exist. I had never uttered these words before I said them to the group. Not to John Blackwell, not to myself. Not before I sat down to write this book. Not before I wrote the last chapter. Not until I stood in front of that great group of people to answer their questions.*

*But it was there, I can assure you. Given the aim of our project, it was there, waiting. And then it showed itself to me and we claimed it as ours. For this project. For these special people. For the difference we needed to establish in Manny's mind and heart between what he was learning and what everyone else in the world was learning.*

*How is it possible, you might ask, to create something you have never done? How can the Leader carry out his or her mission if he or she doesn't know what it is? If he or she has never done it before? There is only one way: Imagine it!*

*All that I have been saying to you so far in this book is the product of my imagination. The imagination is the heart of the*

(continued)

*Dreamer. Your imagination is the heart of your life and what you do with it. You are being called upon to be a Hero without any training to be a Hero. You are being called upon to be a Leader without any training to be a Leader.*

*Your imagination is the key to unlock the door of your entrepreneurial spirit. Conjuring up your energy, your spirit, your passion for your cause is the only worthy aim of a fully committed human being. What you are being evoked to invent is the mission of your lifetime!*

# 24

## The Mission Reveals Itself

Like every writer, I am asked where my work originates,
and if I knew I would go there more often to find more.

—Arthur Miller

We have conjured up out of an empty space no bigger than an atom and as large as the universe, the Great Idea I call *A Course for Heroes!*

Do you see what we're coming to here? The Dreaming doesn't stop when the Thinker takes on the Dream. It just intensifies with the force of the Thinker's hot mind. The Dreaming doesn't stop when the Storyteller takes over, either. It becomes instead incarnated in the Magic of the spellbinder's Words. The Dreaming doesn't stop when the Leader takes over. Instead, it very quickly becomes a powerful sword.

The Dream is the thing, dear reader. It is. And if you need any more proof than I've just given you, you have been sleeping through this Story in the hope of something more substantial, when only the least substantial will do. The least substantial to me is an Idea that has no proof. But, instead, has great whimsy. Sings and trots. Calls to your muse. An idea like the one just mentioned, *A Course for Heroes*—whoever heard of such a thing?!

No such thing had ever been done before!

And that's exactly the point!

■

Not too long after our group meeting, John Blackwell and I met again, this time at a nearby coffee shop. He was waiting for me when I arrived, and was already nursing a cup of coffee.

"Good morning, John," I said. "And how's our hero this morning?"

"Good morning, Michael," John answered. "We've got a lot to talk about and a whole lot more to do. And, our hero is fine. Just fine. He's just a bit confused."

"Tell me about it," I responded.

It took us about two hours to get through it all. John Blackwell described to me what occurred at the meeting after they reconvened. There were many questions, 99 percent of which were about how the *Manny Espinosa Project* was going to be implemented.

The developers asked one set of questions; the restaurant managers asked an entirely different set. The developers were interested in the process; the managers were interested in the problems associated with introducing a new concept into their operating units. Overall, however, with the exception of a couple of people who simply left the meeting because they didn't believe in the Project, most were enthusiastic.

The general agreement was that *if* we could develop the curriculum, and *if* we could interest Manny the Kid in participating, and *if* we could sustain Manny the Kid's interest long enough to make a difference in him, and *if* we could produce the bottom line results we intended to produce for the restaurant owner, and *if* we could systematize the course in such a way that relatively ordinary people could deliver it successfully, and if we could do all that and still make money, well, then, we would have ourselves a winner. But, of course, how we were going to fulfill all those "ifs" was a mighty big question. And at what cost? And over how much time? And with how many people?

John finally came to the "confused" part.

"When I say I'm a bit confused, what I really mean to say is that I am not as certain as I usually am. I love to be certain. I feel solid when I'm certain. I don't like to feel confused, but I've come face-to-face with how little I truly understand about what needs to be done to build *A Course for Heroes*. And when that hit me, I asked, 'Am I the guy to do it?' That's where the confusion stepped in. So that's my question for you, Michael: 'Am I the guy to do this thing of yours?'"

I couldn't help but smile. "John, how the hell would I know? I've been asking the same question of myself. How can I even believe that *I'm* the guy to do this? There have to be thousands of guys who are better suited to do this thing than you and I are. But they're not sitting at this table. They weren't running your meeting yesterday. They didn't dream up the idea, and they haven't a clue that we're doing this. If they did, they would probably tell us we're nuts. And they are probably right.

"But, here we are," I continued, "and *you* are the man to do it because you said you would. And *I* am the man to do it because I said I would. We've told too many people to back out now. So, our goose, as they say, is damn well cooked. Do you have any other questions that haven't already been answered by the forces that brought us together?"

John replied, "Only one. How do we do this thing we decided to do?"

■

Developing *A Course for Heroes* was no different than developing a course for anything else. First was the Emotional Content. Second was the Physical Content. Third was the Rational Content. Fourth was the Time. Fifth was the Result.

All five pieces were driven by the student . . . Manny Espinosa!

The emotional maturity or immaturity of the student determined how the Emotional Content was to be organized.

The physical maturity or immaturity of the student determined how the Physical Content was to be organized.

The rational maturity or immaturity of the student determined how the Rational Content was to be organized.

The Time and the Result are driven by each other respectively, and also by the demands placed upon them by the content of the three components of the Course.

The entire System would only work if all of its five components were created to work as one whole, as opposed to five separate things. The "one whole thing" in *A Course for Heroes*, of course, was Manny Espinosa. We were creating this Course just for him. If one were to construct a scale from one to ten for our candidates' emotional, physical, and rational maturity, we would hazard a guess (using our intuition) that it would be on the lower end in all three.

Without any testing (which would take time and money and would more than likely unnecessarily alienate Manny), it would be safer if we built the Course to the lower end of the scale, because it would be more inclusive that way, rather than toward the higher end of the scale, which would exclude the largest number of Mannys. The Course's success depends on its ability to touch as many Mannys as possible.

Of course, once touched, it was equally predictable that not all

Mannys would be successful. We could not determine in advance what the success ratio would be, but we could hazard a guess (again, using our intuition) that likely more than 30 percent would drop out before completing the Course, and another 20 percent would fail to continue with the Course throughout the stages following Graduation from the Intensive. This left a success rate of 50 percent.

A success rate of 50 percent would have a profoundly positive impact on not only the community of Manny Espinosas in the United States, but upon their families, their peers, their communities, their employers, and the country as a whole.

While a 50 percent success rate might indicate that we also have a 50 percent failure rate, this is not necessarily true. The Mannys who leave the project will have received training and support unlike any they have ever been given. All Mannys will be indelibly changed by the experiences they have in the *Manny Espinosa Project*, whether they graduate or not. And that is our aim.

So, to build *A Course for Heroes*, all of the curriculum components must be developed to fit Manny's emotional, physical, and rational needs if they are to have a positive impact on him. Emotionally, Physically, Rationally will be the context from now on.

We reached another very important conclusion: no classrooms. *A Course for Heroes* designed to transform the life of Manny Espinosa will not be taught in a classroom. Manny likely only has negative associations with the classroom. Manny also only has negative associations with classroom teachers.

So, then what? How do we teach Manny if he's not sitting at a desk?

I envision a martial arts course where Manny is sitting on the floor in front of his Sensei. I see a swimming pool where Manny is in the water being taught by a trainer. I visualize Manny with a laptop computer, or in a gym, or in a park. I can picture Manny taking a course on survival in the desert. I just can't see him sitting in a class-room.

■

"And that's the way you will do it, John." I said. "You will simply begin. You will look at the one you are determined to touch, Manny Espinosa, and you will build *A Course for Heroes* the best way you can, given the expertise available to you, by knowing that the truth lives in Manny. Until he does what he is absolutely going to do, the only thing you know is what you *think* he's going to do."

■

To build the curriculum for *A Course for Heroes*, we need to start at the beginning. The skills we have already determined Manny the Hero needs to possess are emotional, physical, and rational. Manny needs to be emotionally committed, physically committed, and rationally committed to the Dream, Vision, Purpose, and Mission of *Who Is Manny Espinosa?*

But the emotional, physical, and rational crucible for Manny's development are really a platform for all the other more tactical skills he must learn over time. They—emotional, physical, rational—are what we will call Core Level Skills.

The skills we called concentration, discrimination, organization, innovation, and communication are what we will call Secondary Level Skills.

The skills we would identify as speaking, reading, writing, and so forth, we would call Tertiary Level Skills.

So, we now have identified three wheels of learning in a Hierarchy of Skills we are calling *A Course for Heroes*.

"Let's not confuse ourselves too much with the prospect of that," I suggested to John. "Let's just start at the beginning. Manny is an apprentice. What are the Seven Essential Skills he or she needs to develop at this state of *A Course for Heroes* that will enable him to graduate from the Six-Week Intensive and go on to continue his or her education on the job as well as in his or her next stage at *A Course for Heroes*?

"The important point here, John, is that all we need at the beginning of this odyssey is to begin it. The juice, the learning, the improvement will all happen as soon as we're in it!

"Remember, John, McDonald's has a three hundred percent annual attrition rate. How good do we have to be to completely transform it? Remember this, too. Their focus is to teach Manny how to do a job. Our focus is to teach Manny how to become a human being. Which would you bet on if you were a betting man?"

John quickly replied, "I'd bet on Manny."

"Me, too," I agreed. "So let's get started."

# STOP
### AND
# FOCUS

## *The Mission Reveals Itself*

*You are participating in the movement of Dreaming, Thinking, Storytelling, Leading, and Missioneering as it is working its wonderful way into the world. It is happening here as we speak, the evolution of a revolution that occurs in real time.*

*What did you think happens in the minds of imagineers? Did you suppose that invention is an arcane and scientific process, a mathematical deliberation that occurs over time, similar to the creation of stalactites and stalagmites? Drip, drip, drip?*

*Did you think that there is something you need to learn that is cumbersome and weighted down in the classroom where all the experts live to teach? Did you think that method is always linear, always analytical, always a product of education and rumination and expert dialogue?*

*If you thought that, it is no wonder . . . **because you have been taught that.** You have been trained to believe in experts. You have been indoctrinated to believe that expertise is where all understanding lives. You have been trained to believe that experts are authorities, and authorities are experts. And that science is everything.*

*While some experts are authorities, most aren't. Even if they were, the world is invented differently than they would have you believe. Remember, you do not need to have experience in business to invent a great business. When you awaken the entrepreneur within, all hell breaks loose. All joy breaks out. New things are made from old things. Old things are thrown into the garbage. Life will never be the same.*

■

# 25

# We Suddenly Understand

All these things have happened, and probably they will
happen again. I have learned a few tricks along the way, a
few random skills and simple avoidance techniques—but
mainly it has been luck, I think, and a keen attention to
karma, along with my natural girlish charm.

—Hunter S. Thompson, *Kingdom of Fear:*
*Loathsome Secrets of a Star-Crossed Child in the*
*Final Days of the American Century*

As John Blackwell and I worked together to shape the design of
the Company called *Who Is Manny Espinosa?*, we met with developers, restaurant managers, Cadre, and the Mannys themselves, an
increasing number of them, as we began to practice telling the Manny
Espinosa Story.

We met Mannys in malls, in restaurants where they were working, on the street where many were working, in high schools where
we were allowed access as a part of a chamber of commerce initiative
we helped found. Community associations were of great help to us.
They listened to our Story, asked questions about our company, about
me, and about John Blackwell.

The answers we gave them satisfied them, despite the fact that, at this point, all we had was our Story. There was no operating company, nor was there *A Course for Heroes.* Of course, I knew there didn't need to be. It was obvious to everyone we talked to that we were "in process," that the Course was "under development," and that the Dream, Vision, Purpose, and Mission were "under development."

But our passion and commitment were not "under development." It was unmistakably clear that we were not fooling around. The Company called *Who Is Manny Espinosa?* was going to happen.

We practiced telling our Story to the point that either John or I could tell it in our sleep. Each and every time we told our Story, the reality of it became clearer in our minds, our hearts. There was such certainty and clarity in it.

As I listened to John, it was if I were listening to myself, as it was to him when he listened to me. We were brothers under the skin. Both of us committed more deeply to Manny.

Just as I had known thirty years before that I was going to build "the McDonald's of small business consulting," I knew I was going to create *Who Is Manny Espinosa?* It rang an internal bell in me. And you, too, have that bell in you: the entrepreneur within.

Yes, John and I met Manny Espinosa at every opportunity we could. In the beginning it was as tough as we knew it would be. A couple of white guys of our age couldn't have expected it to be any different. Manny didn't trust us. Why should he? But, truthfully, we didn't trust Manny, either. So, we would look at each other at the beginning warily.

But, as we warmed up to the job, as we took turns telling Manny the Story, his defenses began to drop. His interest picked up. He began to ask us questions. The answers we gave him, while not satisfying, were stimulating his interest. He asked more questions, and more questions.

Each time Manny asked us another question, the picture of *A*

*Course for Heroes* took on a new dimension. Our Hero began to take shape as a living Latino or Hispanic human being. Our Hero had a body and formed questions in his mind and expressed them through his mouth. John and I began to see our Hero wake up in Manny Espinosa.

The interviews increased in number and in intensity. As they did, the Story altered itself in many ways that configured themselves into an even more cogent Story, a Story with a Beginning, a Middle, and an End. Just like this Story has. A Story meant to be told to large numbers of Mannys, which was critical if we were to grow *Who Is Manny Espinosa?*, the Company.

The Story became, over a very short period of time, the *Manny Espinosa* Seminar. The Seminar very quickly turned into the Lead Generation System that was essential to the success of the Company. And John and I worked on the Seminar to the point where either he or I could deliver it once a week, twice a week, or even three times a day, if it was required.

The bilingual Seminar was called:

*Making It on Your Own in America*
*. . . if You're Young, Hispanic, and Broke*
*A Seminar for Hispanics between the ages of sixteen and twenty-four*

The seminar was presented in English, with Spanish translation provided.

John and I would take turns doing the first Seminars until we had it scripted to the point where we could audition, train, and replace ourselves with other contract Presenters, preferably, but not necessarily, Hispanics.

We continued interviewing Mannys and adjusting the Seminar script to the point where we knew exactly what we needed to do to draw Manny to the *Manny Espinosa* Recruitment & Development Center in the heart of San Diego. There, we provided our recruits with a firsthand experience called *An Introduction to a Course for Heroes.*

We scheduled our first Introduction three weeks away, at the YMCA, where we had rented a hall. That meant that, between now and then, we had to hold our first *Making It on Your Own in America* Seminar and get a large number of Mannys to attend it.

We hired a bunch of young Hispanic kids to take *Manny Espinosa* leaflets to every store, restaurant, and meeting hall in the primarily Hispanic neighborhoods in San Diego. The handout said:

*FREE SEMINAR for YOUNG HISPANICS.*
*Parents invited to attend.*
*Making It on Your Own in America . . .*

and then described the Seminar. One side was in English; the other in Spanish.

The Seminar was to be held in a local church on Sunday afternoon, as gang activity was less likely if we held our seminars in churches.

On the other hand, there was the possibility that Manny would think this was a church-sponsored event and therefore associate *Manny Espinosa* with the many other church-sponsored development programs in the community. This was an association we wanted to avoid. Ours was a profit-driven business, and we wanted everyone to know it was a profit-driven business. If *we* didn't know how to make money and grow a hugely successful company, how could we possibly teach Manny to do it?

But, for the first Seminar, we didn't need to test our ability to attract Manny to the Seminar. We wanted to test our ability to convert a reasonable percentage of the Mannys who showed up to our Seminar to sign up for our *Introduction to a Course for Heroes* the following week.

With the Lead Generation Program under way, we focused our attention on getting ready for a successful Seminar. We had to make certain that the Introduction produced the result it was intended to produce: enrollments in our first *A Course for Heroes* Intensive. We needed exactly seventy Mannys enrolled in our first Intensive.

Here's how the money was supposed to work. An Intensive lasts six weeks. If, as projected, only 70 percent of those enrolled were to graduate (which means forty-nine graduates) and we were to place all forty-nine in entry-level positions at $3,000 each, that means the Intensive would produce $147,000 in First Line Revenue. We also were projecting Second Line Revenue from government grants of $150 per enrollee, for a total of $7,500 per Intensive, or total Gross Revenue for each, for a total of $927,000 per six Intensives, placing 294 Graduates every two months, for a total of 1,764 Graduates per year in one Recruitment & Development Center for annual gross revenue of $5,562,000.

The total annual cost for operating a *Manny Espinosa* Recruitment & Development Center was calculated to be roughly $4,000,000, for a pretax profit of $1,562,000. These costs not only included the cost of delivering the Intensives, but ongoing training and support as well following the Intensives for all Graduates.

Each Graduate was also invited to become a Cadre in training, for which he or she paid a slight fee, in addition to the fees each Graduate was expected to pay for their continuing training following Graduation and placement in their first Employer School.

All Graduates were invited to attend courses as we developed them, all intended to intensify Manny's sense of responsibility and accountability for his or her own future and the life of his or her community. All critical in *A Course for Heroes*. All critical if we were to produce the result we intended to produce on Manny's behalf and on behalf of the Company called *Who Is Manny Espinosa?*

And the Dream went on.

▪

We held our first *Manny Espinosa* Seminar three weeks later. It was a rousing success, attended by hundreds of young Hispanics, their parents, and other members of the community, as well as representatives from numerous employers.

John and I drew straws to determine who was to deliver our very first *Manny Espinosa* Seminar, and I won. What an extraordinary Seminar it was! I have never had a more suspicious audience, or a more attentive one. Everyone in that audience wanted to believe in what I was saying to them. They wanted to believe that there was a new way for Hispanic children to grow up in the America they lived in. They wanted to believe in the American Dream, in capitalism, in the idea of a liberty that was available to each and every Hispanic kid growing up in the barrio.

The Seminar lasted the full three hours. And when I was done they gave me a rousing ovation. Our team was seated at a long string of tables at the back of the church waiting to sign up participants for our *Introduction to a Course for Heroes*. We were immediately swamped with applications. I looked around for John. He was surrounded by a large number of restaurant executives and association leaders. He was having the time of his life!

# STOP

## AND

# FOCUS

# We Suddenly Understand

*"We suddenly understand" is not something that occurs only once, as a singular, solitary event. It occurs as the process of Dreaming moves forward.*

*We suddenly understand that there is no way out of this thing we have invented, if there ever was, because it is alive!*

*Yes, it is alive! And you gave birth to it! And it is now yours to feed, to nurture, to love, to teach. This is for real, and you've created it. So, here at this special place to focus, ask yourself this very important question: "Am I taking myself seriously yet?"*

*Don't rush to answer it, no. Just stop for a moment and focus. And then ask it again: are you taking yourself seriously yet? Do you catch my drift?*

*If you had to stand before hundreds of Hispanic kids and their families who came to a place for only one reason . . . to discover whether they could take you seriously . . . what would you think at that moment? "Am I actually going to do what I just prom-*

*(continued)*

*ised them I am going to do? Or am I simply going to write a book about it?"*

*What would you do, dear reader? Would you dig down deep? To awaken the entrepreneur within, you must take this wondrous part of yourself seriously—step out and make some lives something they shouldn't have to live without.*

■

# 26

## The Mission Is Being Realized

Find your risk and you will find yourself.
Sometimes that means leaving your home,
your father's house, and your birthplace, and traveling
to strange lands. Both the biblical Abraham and the
Buddha do this quite literally. But for the cabbalist the
true journey does not require dramatic breaks with past
and home. It is rather a journey of the imagination.

—Marc Gafni, *The Mystery of Love*

Thirteen days and counting. A Dream is on its way. Thirteen days and the Cadre is bursting with training, with preparation for the introduction to *A Course for Heroes*. Will they be ready? Only John Blackwell and the Developers know the final truth. But, then, if we were honest with ourselves, we would all say not one of us knows. We can only *feel* it. And the feeling was all good.

I stood up to address the group.

"Well, ladies and gentlemen, it looks like we're exactly where we need to be. You are clearly ready for takeoff. I've been watching you run through your Introduction to the Course, and in my estimation, you've truly nailed it every single time. I'm certain Manny will respond exactly as we want him to. I can't imagine anything other than complete success.

"To you Developers, I can only say you have touched the heart of the Hero we're trying to create. This thing you've built is like no training I have ever done or seen done. How you pulled it off with so little time simply astounds me. Thank you for your incredible demonstration of heroic work in action. You are all Heroes as far as I am concerned.

"And John, thank you from the bottom of my heart. You have done what you said you would do. And for that I am deeply grateful. But, even more than that, through it all you have remained steadfast to the rules of the game we agreed to. You are one of the few men in my life I can say that about. You are more than you said you would be when we first met. You are undoubtedly a Hero, First Class.

"So, let's get started. Fill me in on where we are with our Strategy and Plan."

■

Following the meeting, John Blackwell and I spent some time discussing the status of the upcoming *Introduction*. We had over ninety Mannys coming to it, far more than we expected. Far more than we needed. The question we now saw wasn't whether we could interest Manny in our Program, but how to limit the number of Mannys who wanted to enroll in it, so that the group would be manageable.

"We're ahead of the game, John. Tell me how that feels."

"It feels just as you must imagine it feels, Michael. I'm blown away by how far we've come, and concerned that it's been so easy. The enrollment has been easy, the development has been easy, the recruitment of Cadre has been easy, the recruitment of restaurant partners has been easy. What are we missing? That's the question that keeps coming up for me. Life isn't supposed to be this easy. And if it's been this easy, why hasn't anyone else thought about doing it? With restaurant attrition rates being what they are, why hasn't the restaurant industry done this? With the proliferation of the Hispanic population being what it is, why hasn't the government done this? With the extreme amount of political activity focused on the emergence of the Hispanic consciousness in the country, why haven't all the not-for-profit organizations in this niche done it? What are we missing, Michael? You and I can't be that smart that we've identified a problem and a solution that nobody else in the universe has failed to identify. Doesn't it make you nervous?"

I thought for a moment. "You know, John, normally I'm the one who runs that number in my own mind. What's missing in this picture is a question I ask all the time. But, for whatever reason, this time it never occurred to me, and I'll tell you why. Somebody once said 'there is nothing new under the sun.' A client of mine in the early, early years said it another way. He said, 'new things get old.' However you think about it, all we've done with *Manny*, the Company, is to reorganize the pieces of the world into a pattern that nobody thought to do before.

"In short, the rule of the world is that *everybody does what everybody does.* They might do it differently, but they do the very same thing. And that's what makes Manny so original; we're doing something nobody has done, but had to *be* done, and that's why it's so easy. Because we're doing exactly the right thing, for exactly the right reason, in exactly the right way. We're building a Brand. And, once we do it, you better believe it that everyone is going to jump on the wagon. But, by then, with the grace of God, we will have built our *Course for Heroes* so well, with such intensity, no one will be able to compete with us. We're right at that stunningly alive place where what we are doing is exactly what needs to be done."

■

Readers, do you see why I am so enthralled with this game called entrepreneurship, and the many forms it can take?

First, Manny Espinosa is just a name picked out of an emotional hat. And then Manny Espinosa became an entire course of study—a growth opportunity bigger than life. A great idea, one of the greatest. A way of being, a way of knowing, a way of reaching a huge number of human beings and transforming their relationships with themselves and their world. How big is that, to populate your life and your world with a cause in the form of an enterprise that you could pour yourself into endlessly? And so easily done.

I sat at my computer and spoke to myself and to you. I wrote to myself and to you. As I did, all of the voices spoke through me. All the pictures revealed themselves to me.

You could have done that as well as I did! This, all of it, is a product of desire. It is a product of Love. It was, and is, a product of Imagination. This, all of it, is a gift from God, a movement of energy, which is discovered by giving myself up to it as I'm giving myself up to you. You could have done it all! You still can. You can begin right now, as I take you through one more step—the step I call *the Revelation of the Golden Pyramid.*

# STOP
### AND
# FOCUS

## The Mission Is Being Realized

*Throughout our journey together in this book, I have attempted to serve as your entrepreneurial guide.*

*I went from one world into a completely different world when we visited the Leader and the Mission and Manny Espinosa. Prior to that, I shared with you historical information about The Michael Thomas Corporation, E-Myth Worldwide, and In the Dreaming Room.*

*Then we wandered off to take a journey in the Dreaming World, with me as your Chief Dreamer, to demonstrate how Intentional Dreaming is actually done. Even while the Mission is forming itself in the Leader's mind. Even as John Blackwell, my surrogate COO, took the Mission on, even though it was all being created in my imagination—and in my heart and my mind.*

*As I faced the obstacles I would necessarily be forced to deal with in the course of inventing* Who Is Manny Espinosa? *the Company, I wrote my way out of them—in my mind, in my sense of play, in my joyful relationship with the problems I was confronting, the unknowns I was facing, and the personalities I was dealing with and inventing.*

*The entrepreneur does that, you know. You get to do that, as well.*

*(continued)*

*What could be more satisfying than knowing, as I know now, that the Company I call* Who Is Manny Espinosa? *is as real and as present as the coffee shop next door?*

*That's what happens when the entrepreneur wakes up. The world wakes up with him or her. And you, yes, you, are the creator of all that. Hosanna and by God, what an extraordinary gift it is to us all!*

# 27

## The Revelation
## of the Golden Pyramid

The ultimate aim was for every human being
to be immensely creative.

—Norman Mailer, *On God*

We are now at the end of our Journey, and have seen a dream or two take place. But now, dear reader, we have to get down to the basics. And I promise you that's exactly what we'll do after I've told you another extraordinary tale.

■

We are awakening the Entrepreneur within you to build a unique Enterprise. An "Enterprise" is a very large company. It will be large, because nothing else will satisfy the Entrepreneur in you. It will be unique because that is what entrepreneurs do. "Unique" means it does something no one else does, or it does something in a way no one else does it.

But, you have to start from where you are. And where you are right now is an Economy of One. There is just you. And that is where the Golden Pyramid begins; with you, just you, an Economy of One. You are inventing a new company. You are "In the Dreaming Room." You have nothing but your Imagination and a blank piece of paper in front of you, and "a little man in a white suit and a pink tie with a sharp stick" to keep you company.

That's me! And we're going on a journey together. We're going on a Dreaming Journey in pursuit of the impossible. We're intent upon waking up the voice in you, the voice that has been trying to speak to you for as long as you've lived. A voice that probably spoke to you many, many times when you were a child, but which you stopped listening to so many years ago, when you stopped being interested in childish things. When you discovered the Truth about Santa Claus and Christmas, the Easter Bunny and the Easter egg hunt. When you discovered the Truth about the Tooth Fairy. That's when the voice of dreaming was taken away from you. That's when you stopped listening to it.

But, did anyone tell you that the Truth you were told was not the Truth? That the Truth you were told was intended to wake you up, so you would become a practical person in the Real World? The Real World of work, where you have to make a living? The Real World where kids don't live?

Did anybody ever tell you that? Of course not. Because they didn't know enough to tell you that. They were told the very same thing!

I am telling you now that the Real World sucks! It's the invention of an unplayful mind. It's the invention of old people! It's the invention of people who work for a living! It's the invention of control.

But we're in the Dreaming Room now. We are not focusing on Old Co., the company you've got, the life you've got. We're playing in the World of Make Believe, where everything is possible, especially the impossible. You and I are sitting here with a blank piece of paper.

■

The Revelation of the Golden Pyramid is the fact that from one you can invent one hundred. From one Practice you can invent one Enterprise. One medical practice times one hundred. One massage practice times one hundred. One plumbing practice, website practice, or personal training practice times one hundred. One hundred times you—you, doing something unique or uniquely.

One hundred times you doing something uniquely is McDonald's, Starbucks, or Wal-Mart. It is the first airplane, the first television, the first business coach, the first fax machine, the Internet.

What is your way of doing something that's been done so many times before but is dying to be done in a more effective way than anyone had ever considered? What is your reprogramming of the world?

It's all there on that blank piece of paper, waiting to reveal itself. It's all there inside your imagination waiting to come alive in a word, in two words, in three words. Listen. Draw. Write!

■

Let me help it along. Imagine that you are a massage therapist and don't really want to create a large business. All you want to do is practice massage. All you want is enough clients to make a good living and enjoy what you do.

Play with me here just a little bit. All you want is just a little bit more. But wait. Why did you become a massage therapist at the very beginning?

There could have been several reasons. You might have been out of work and somebody suggested you go to school to learn a trade. And the vocational school catalogue offered A (Accounting) to Z (Zebra training), but somewhere in the middle of the M's the words *massage therapist* showed up and you had just had a massage and re-membered how good it felt. So, someone or something in you popped up and said, "Yes!"

So, you went to massage school and learned about the benefits of massage. Your clients while in school told you how wonderful you were. And you experienced the true joy that comes from doing some-thing you enjoy doing, doing something that provided value to the people you did it for, and doing something that people truly loved you for and gave you all kinds of acknowledgment for as a result.

You opened your practice in your home and you went to work, believing in the good work you were doing, work that gave you such pleasure and joy, and believing that you were now independently em-ployed and would never, ever, have to go on a job interview again!

However, after a bit of time you began to experience the difficulty of getting new clients and keeping the clients you had, and of mak-ing a reasonable living and paying the bills. You began to experience the frustration that, no matter how hard you tried, you couldn't con-trol the times your clients wanted to see you, or where they wanted to see you.

Because you needed the money, you worked odd hours in odd places, lugging your massage table with you wherever you went: through the snow, in the rain, in the cold, early in the morning, late at night, on weekends, at times you never would have worked before. Does this sound familiar to you? It really doesn't matter if you are a massage therapist, a chiropractor, an auto mechanic, a webmaster, or any other technician suffering from an entrepreneurial seizure.

Does this sound familiar to you, dear reader? Well it should, or, if it doesn't, it will. Because as I've written in every *E-Myth* book, it is the sin of the technician going into business thinking he or she is ac-tually creating a business when in fact he or she is creating the worst job in the world, working for a lunatic! (Yes, that's you!)

So, here we are at the beginning of the Golden Pyramid! Here we are at the Revelation, at that moment where I am going to bring "the Secret" to you.

Are you ready?

Here it is: *There is no secret!*

There is, instead, this grand thing standing there looking at you!

It is huge! It is your future. It is the simple act upon a simple fact.

All you need to do is build one single uniquely practiced practice and you have reinvented your world!

Just!

Like!

That!

The Revelation of the Golden Pyramid is that you can start your revolution from exactly where you are. In fact, you can't start it from anywhere other than where you are. You can start your revolution being exactly who you are, doing exactly what you do. Being a technician suffering from an entrepreneurial seizure. But, with a very big difference. This time, rather than simply going to work *in* your Practice, you are going to go to work *on* your Practice (I have said this at E-Myth countless millions of times) to begin to construct your Golden Pyramid.

This revolution will do four things for you:

1. It will free you from the endless routine of "doing it, doing it, doing it," just to get by.

2. It will teach you exactly what you need to learn in order to build a great company, to invent New Co., one single productive learning step at a time.

3. It will provide you with the Golden Keys to emotional, physical, rational, and spiritual wealth beyond your wildest imagination. (No, this is not Donald Trump stuff,

God forbid! This is Spirit Stuff, Soul Stuff, and, yes, you heard it before . . . this is *Hero* Stuff!)

4. It will awaken the entrepreneur within you, again and again and again, until it is literally impossible for the entrepreneur within you ever to go to sleep again.

■

You want to awaken the entrepreneur within. You want to liberate yourself from doing it, doing it, doing it. You have been to the Dreaming Room. You are earnestly dreaming. You are formulating your Dream, your Vision, your Purpose, your Mission.

You are committed. You are seriously dreaming. You want to invent a company that's scalable (like a highly systematized franchise is), and that's transformational (makes a huge difference of Good in the world). You don't have enough money to do it. You don't have enough imagination yet to do it. You don't have the knowledge to do it. But, you are committed to do it.

What to do, what to do, what to do? Welcome to the Golden Pyramid Strategy for growing a world-class company with only the skills, the capital, the knowledge at hand. We're about to do the impossible. As I said, follow the bouncing ball.

## THE GOLDEN PYRAMID STRATEGY

1) **Identify Old Co.** The skills that you possess are all you have. What are they? What are you able to do that others would buy from you?

2) **Make a list of every single vertical niche market (customer) you could conceivably provide your service to.** These then become your Customer Categories.

3) **Identify your Trading Zone:** the geographical area

within which the majority of your customers live. (In a restaurant, that might be everyone within no more than ten minutes' drive from your location.)

4) **Pick the ten most appealing Customer Categories.** (Overweight people. Diabetics. People who drive high-end automobiles. People who walk to work. Adult illiterates. People who prepare their own tax returns.)

5) **Pick the one most appealing Customer Category.** You are now going to focus all your remaining attention on this one Customer Category. You are going to pick this Customer Category for any number of compelling reasons. Such reasons are:

   a) It is a growing niche market.

   b) It demonstrates a compelling unfulfilled need.

   c) You already are an expert in this niche market.

   d) It is a sizeable market segment with no sign of weakening or diminishing in size.

   e) It is a national market segment with large enough numbers in a significant number of trading zones to warrant national expansion.

   f) It has demonstrated an interest in your core capability.

   g) It has not been identified by potential competitors as a viable niche market. A market that suits every one of the above could for example be diabetics; overweight kids; green-conscious consumers; consumers over age eighty; consumers between the ages of seventy and seventy-five, and so forth.

6) **Learn everything you can possibly learn about this one Customer Category.** Make a list of everything you need to know. Again, Everything. You are going to be the only

person in your kind of business who knows everything you know about this Customer Category. You are going to study, study, study your Customer Category. You will know what it feels like to be your customer, what it feels like to get up in the morning and go to work, what it feels like at work, and what it feels like on the way home from work. You will know where they live, what their home is like, how they furnish their home, what foods they eat, what clothes they wear, who their friends are, and what their friends do. You will know what their politics are, what their religious affiliations are or aren't, and what kind of vehicle they drive. You will understand what's important to them and what frustrates them. Let me say that once again. You will know what frustrates them, what their psychological reality is, what medications they're on, and how often they go to the doctor. And on and on and on. Remember, all this is important to you. You have to learn, learn, learn as though you were going to write a doctoral thesis on this most important customer for this Practice you are about to build . . . just for them. Just for Manny Espinosa. Just for Joe Nation. Just for Donny Dyslexic. Just for this person whose life doesn't work. That's your job—to make his or her life work in your own inimitable, self-styled, extraordinarily unique way.

7) **Design your Client Fulfillment System.** Design it from the front to the back, from the very first customer contact to the very last customer contact, all the way through your relationship with them. Design your Client Fulfillment System visually, emotionally, functionally, and financially. We can all do this. All we need to do is to dig

down deep into the experience, your customer's experience, the visual experience, the emotional experience, the functional experience, the financial experience. Design your Client Fulfillment System to keep the promise your practice was designed to fulfill for your very special customer, the one you know better than anyone else does. Design it with care, with empathy, with love, with concern. Design it as though your life depended upon it. Design it as though there were going to be tens of thousands of these little Practices throughout the world, wherever there are a sufficient number of your special central demographic model consumer to support your very special practice. As though you were building McDonald's, or Starbucks, or Wal-Mart. (You are, whether or not you believe you are!) The heart of your difference will lie at the heart of your practice. You are inventing a unique and lovely experience for just one person: your very special customer. Design every single little piece of this intricate Practice puzzle. Take it apart and put it together again. Do that many, many times. And then you're ready.

8) **Design your Lead Conversion System.** Lead Conversion is what happens when a *lead* (a prospective customer who has expressed an interest in what you do) shows up at your door. You must be ready for him/her! That's why you have done all the work of preparing your Client Fulfillment System, which you've been practicing. You must be ready for them! This is your Lead Conversion System. It includes the script you have prepared, memorized, and practiced again and again to make certain that when that prospective customer walks in your door, or you walk in

his or hers, you are ready for whatever he or she might say or not say to make certain the sale is completed. Do not forget this: your prospective client does not need to be convinced; she needs to be cared for. How you do that is what constitutes your Lead Conversion System. Write it, practice it, complete it, test it. It's the only way you will build one that works. Once it works, it's worth its weight in gold.

9) **Design your Lead Generation System.** You are about to make a promise to your prospective customers. You know who they are, you know where they live (within your trading zone), you know what frustrates them, you know what they want, you've designed your service just for them and only them. Now you are going to pick the words to tell them all that as eloquently and directly and simply as you can. You are telling them (selling them!) that you have solved their problem in a way no one else has (true!), and that you want them to experience your special solution to their unique problem! You have marshaled all of your resources (immense resources!) to make it possible for them to benefit from this effortless trip to your Practice (no work at all), at a time when it is easiest (low traffic) in a way that's convenient (you'll even pick them up and take them home again) for a cost that is insignificant to produce a result they will love (name it, exactly) for only one reason (there has to be one, which is your motivation, and it has to make sense . . . the rational armament to support the emotional conclusion), and it's being done for a limited time only (we just moved in; we can't afford to do this too many times; my mother made me promise; I'm not crazy!). Lead Genera-

tion is anything you do from leaflets left in mailboxes, to emails, to a speech at the local churches, to running downtown stark naked with a sign hanging from your neck, saying, "Please visit me, please visit me, I'm lonely!" You get my point. Lead Generation becomes a System once it has been validated to work better than anything else you've tried, and then you work it, and work it, and work it, until it stops working, or until the reason it worked (Grand Opening) has worn out its usefulness. (You obviously can't continue to promote your Grand Opening six months after you've opened, no matter how enthusiastic you are about opening your business!)

10) **Test the effectiveness of your new Practice.** There is only one way to test the effectiveness of your new Practice, and that's by doing it. But, to do that you must set up your Marketing Management System, called CRM (Customer Relationship Management) in the vernacular. Your CRM will tell you how many prospects responded to your Lead Generation actions, who they are, where they are (their contact information), what they wanted, what action was taken (yours and theirs), what the result was (*if* they bought, when they bought, whether the transaction was completed), how much they spent, and so on. As you review this information every day, you'll become more familiar with the Truth about your Practice. (For more about acquiring your Golden Pyramid CRM, come to www.awakeningtheentrepreneur.com.) But, the real Truth about your Practice is what you experience in the operation of it every day in all of the functions you fill at the beginning—the sole salesperson, the sole practitioner (message therapist, cardiologist, ac-

countant, bookkeeper, auto repair person, and so forth). You will also be the chief marketing officer, the chief executive officer, the chief financial officer, and so on. Each of these accountabilities has a specific point of view, both from the top of the Golden Pyramid as well as from the base and the middle of the Golden Pyramid. Each perspective is important toward the evolution of your Journey toward the completion of the Golden Pyramid, the evolution of your Practice to your Business to your Enterprise. The job you're doing now is the most important job you will ever be called to do: designing, building, and replicating the Practice that is the DNA of your Business and of the Enterprise that is its conclusion. Does your Practice work? If not, why not? The amazing thing is that rarely will the Practice be so off, so wrong, that it has to be scrapped. If you've done the work of getting to know your Customer as we've discussed earlier, if you've prepared your Practice with what you've learned about your Customer, if you've tested your Lead Generation and Lead Conversion actions rigorously, and if you've practiced, rehearsed your Practice diligently, it will work ninety-nine times out of one hundred. Your Customer will want what you've decided to build for him or her; all you've got to do is stay with it until it works like a little Swiss watch. And it will! It wants to! You're there for a very good reason. You are determined to make a difference. And you are determined to scale it so that many, many people can benefit from your decision. Your practice will work. No doubt about it. So, now, you're ready to scale it.

11) **Document your Practice.** You now know exactly how to

generate a lead, convert that lead into revenue, and deliver your service or product. Document the entire System as if it were a franchise, as if you were creating an operations manual for someone else to do exactly what you have successfully done. You are not looking for someone to replace you, you are looking for someone to do what you have learned how to do. You are intending to hand off your Practice to another. Your Practice is your intellectual property. Your Practice is a set of processes (systems employed over time) that work consistently to produce as close to an identical result as possible. Your intellectual property is worth a lot of money. You have invested a lot of time, intelligence, patience, and determination into its development, all to bring you to this point in time, where you are preparing the operations manual for your practice successor to use your intelligent, expert system (that's what your IP is!) so you can begin to expand your reach. One Practice is an economy of one. Two Practices are an economy of two. Three Practices are an economy of three. And one hundred Practices are an economy of one hundred. The way to get from an economy of one to an economy of one hundred is very, very simple. But, first, you need to Document Your Practice: That's Job One.

12) **Create your Surrogate Practitioner Agreement.** Before you recruit your Surrogate Practitioner, you need to create your Practitioner Agreement. See a trademark/ patent/copyright attorney to complete this Agreement, along with an employment attorney to make certain it abides by the appropriate laws in your domain. Remember, you are about to establish the template for all future

surrogate practitioner relationships. If your intellectual property is to be protected, and if your future relationships are to be built on understanding and trust, you must take this step carefully. This is a very important step, so you either must choose your law providers carefully, or utilize the basic agreements I have already provided for this purpose at www.awakeningtheentrepreneur .com.

13) **Recruit your first Surrogate Practitioner.** Your Surrogate Practitioner is someone just like you who wants to do what you have already done. To prepare her own Vertical Market Strategy is going to take the same amount of practice it took you to create yours. Your advantage is that you have now developed the expertise to do it by doing it. That is worth a great deal to your SP. However, once she has learned what you know, she will not be satisfied simply working for a living in your Practice; she wants to grow as you are doing. Therein lies a significant secondary opportunity for you in your status as an Intentional Dreamer as well as a significant opportunity for your many Surrogate Practitioners as you recruit them and train them to become experts in the use of your System. Imagine that each new Surrogate Practitioner will pay you to train them to become an expert in your System, while generating reasonable income doing the work, both for you and for themselves. Second, imagine your Surrogate Practitioners learning through their expert use of your System, how the Golden Pyramid works in practice, so much so that they see the opportunity to build their own Vertical Market System in the same industry as you, or in a different, but allied, indus-

try. As they become interested through the In the Dreaming Room process in combination with their firsthand experience in your System, they will more than likely wish to partner with you and your already successfully emerging Enterprise to design and build their Practice. Of course, should they wish to do that, one of the requirements will be for them to assist you in recruiting, training, and monitoring the performance of their Surrogate Practitioner to replace themselves in your System. As this occurs, over and over again (as it will since you, by your very nature and practice, will be awakening the entrepreneur within each and every practitioner you attract to your Company), you can begin to see how the energy from your entrepreneurial venture will begin to stimulate the energy in many more entrepreneurial ventures, creating work for many practitioners of your category, more customers receiving significantly better service than they ever have before, as your economy of one morphs into an economy of three, ten, fifty, and more. So, your recruitment process must be developed into a System as well, called: Let Me Tell You the Story of the Golden Pyramid. Or, how one inexperienced person can design, build, and grow one extraordinary company on his or her own, without any capital, any knowledge of business, or any reason to believe it can be done. And that Story is a story you will learn to love and tell, because it is your Story and my Story, and the Story of tens of thousands of extraordinary awakening entrepreneurs the world over. It's a Story that will reinvent the economic reality of the world!

14) **Train your first Surrogate Partner.** This is a rigorous

process, because you are doing it for the very first time, and because your SP will resist it. She or he will resist it because in this increasingly standardless world, most of us are unfamiliar with the demands of rigorous practice. We are unfamiliar with standards and with the notion of meaning, and how the word "meaning" connotes standards, rules, principles, character, ethics, and morality. So, a very clear path needs to be established between each step of the process until they actually are entrusted to work as a paraprofessional, or apprentice, in the delivery of the first benchmark of your service. This System also needs to be built but, fortunately, not *before* you bring your first SP aboard, but *while* you bring him or her aboard. The development of the Process can become a part of the first phase of training through the artful use of "case practices." A case practice is a Story line in which you posit hypothetical circumstances that the Surrogate Practitioner is being asked to diagnose or asked to provide a solution for. The solutions or diagnoses then become opportunities for Socratic dialogue, questions that pose quandaries that the diagnoses or solutions have yet to effectively respond to. In any case, the training process through which you replace yourself with a willing and inspired Surrogate Practitioner provides you with many opportunities for improvement, not only of the Practice and the Client Fulfillment System of the Practice, but also your relationship with it. There is nothing more contributive to the improvement of your Practice than when you bring new people aboard.

15) **Build your Business Management System.** As you replicate your practice, you will move up into the Business of

which your Practices are the aggregate components. To do that calls for a Business Management System. For more about your Business Management System, go to www.awakeningtheentrepreneur.com. Your Business Management System has three objectives: 1) to monitor the performance of your Practices; 2) to improve the operating systems of your Practices as they are; and 3) to continually expand the capability of your Practices to rise beyond their current core competence. In 1) your Business Management System provides you, the business manager, with the information you require to make strategic and tactical decisions concerning the management of the Practices and the leadership of the Business. Number 2) provides you with the synoptic understanding of the Business as a whole, how well the Practices are providing the uniformity of result needed to establish the awareness, acceptance, and preference of your brand of service to your customer, and your Company's ability to sustain that mind-set by its ability to do what it does in the way it is intended to do it. The purpose of 3) is to provide you, the business manager, with the awareness of shifts taking place in the market represented by your special customer, and how you are being called upon to deal with it successfully.

16) **Replicate your Business.** Now that your Business Management System is doing the job it was intended to do, now that you know what you need to know about the co-efficiency of your multiple Practices, and now that you know your Business has the ability to operate multiple Practices with brand integrity, the time has come to replicate your Business. If one business is the aggregate of

ten Practices (call it a District), then ten businesses are the aggregate of one hundred Practices, an Enterprise, which in a world of Enterprises becomes the Region. But, at the scale we're working on, the Enterprise is all there is—a world in which all parts work simultaneously to produce a beautifully predictable result for everyone involved. It all started as an economy of one, and was built to an economy of one hundred. It is a stunningly productive entrepreneurial System that continues to expand its reach through many alternative models, to transform alternative markets, to enable countless thousands—then millions—of individuals to stretch their entrepreneurial wings by emulating, inventing, exploring, and creating in ways too numerous and too innovative for us to even imagine here and now. And the Golden Pyramid is completed! It was all built on the effectiveness, efficiency, and brand worthiness of a world-class Practice, begun by one, and multiplied one hundred times. The Golden Pyramid is just that. The Enterprise at the apex of the Pyramid. The Ten Businesses at the middle of the Pyramid. And the Practices, all one hundred of them, at the base of the Golden Pyramid.

Welcome to the Age of the New Entrepreneur.
Welcome to the World of Intentional Dreaming!

# All Systems Go!

He wandered far from the accustomed haunts of boys, and
sought desolate places that were in his spirit.

—Mark Twain, *The Adventures of Tom Sawyer*

A number of years ago, I found myself in the middle of Sequoia
National Park in California. I had decided on the spur of the
moment to go to the wilderness to spend some time by myself, with
nothing more than a backpack, my good intentions, and the great
outdoors.

This would not be laughable if I had any previous experience
doing this, but, of course, I didn't. I had never backpacked, either on
my own or with anyone else, in my entire life. I had always thought
somewhat romantically about the notion of getting out there where
the wilderness lived, the place where civilization stopped pressing in
on you, where the busyness of my inner life would come to a stop,
and where the Zen presence I had on many occasions allowed to take
me in, would wash away the noise, lay its calm and quiet hand on my
head, on my chest, on my stomach, and let me feel the healing of Self
come to a rest.

Life at that particular time for me was intense, and I longed for something I couldn't quite put into words; but, for whatever reason, I was called to Sequoia and went willingly, in my car, on my own, to discover what I would discover, with a weekend or four or five days to kill, depending on what happened when I arrived there.

I was fortunate that a cabin was available in the valley, given that I had arrived late in the afternoon when the sun was already on a fast decline behind the mountain to my west. I unpacked the few things I had brought with me: a backpack I had never used, a bunch of things the backpacking expert at the store I went to told me I needed, and as he rang it all up, explained it as best he could to the impetuous, harried man in front of him who must have looked somewhat wild-eyed given the state of mind he was in. I listened to his explanations with the little amount of attention I could spare, figuring that I was going to be gone for no more than five days, and certainly no more than two in the "wilderness"—by this time, the word was beginning to roll off my tongue like *Kleenex,* or *Rolaids,* or *Mercedes* do.

It was as though the word "Wilderness" was quickly becoming a brand of the word "outdoors." You know, first there's the wilderness and then there's everything else. Like "Come to the wilderness where men are men and boys are boys and bears do what bears do." "Are bears a brand, too?" I might have asked myself, being as I was, in one of those scary chatter-scatter moods that sometimes possess me. I had to get the stuff out of the trunk of my car and get to bed in the cabin, which was beginning to shimmer ominously and prophetically in the cold, foreign fading light.

I threw the stuff onto the table in the cabin, fussed around with the potbellied stove and the oak logs the management had put in it, with the paper all ready to light. I struck the industrial-sized match, lit the paper, and the fire began to roar up the metal chimney.

Feeling at least better that I had done something right, I climbed into bed, pulled the covers over me, reached up, and turned out the light, and lay there for about six hours trying to sleep. Tomorrow I was going into the wilderness, which was, as I understood the map the management had given me, someplace up there where the mountains became serious.

Somewhere between that thought and the thought "What are you doing here, Michael Gerber?" I must have fallen asleep.

■

I woke up to the sound of a bird badgering a badger, or was it a badger badgering a bird? Whatever wildlife it was, it was as raucous as a chain saw ripping through wood. I got up, went to the door of the cabin, and opened it to the most glorious fragrance of pine and sawdust, and, well, wilderness smell. I remembered that smell from sometime long ago when, as a boy, I had spent a couple of memorable summer vacations with my parents, brother, and sisters in Yosemite. The smell brought forth all manner of delightful associations that caused me to go back into the cabin, pull out my wilderness stuff, dress, put on my walking boots, strap my backpack to my back, throw my canteen full of water into it, and stride out the front door filled with vinegar, spirit, and purpose. It was seven twenty-five on a beautiful Sunday morning.

■

I traveled up a well-worn path toward what I could only think to be the mountain. I was the only one on the path, but of course that suited me just fine; I was here to be alone. I was here to be on my own. I was here to have a direct communion with the wilderness, with that wild stuff Thoreau wrote about so eloquently, that John Muir made his life's work, that so many poets spent so many impassioned hours of their lives extolling, the place where the Great Spirit within us awoke.

I walked up and up and up, feeling the mountain pulling against the muscles, the tendons, and the bones in both of my legs in unaccustomed ways, my eyes always looking up, my body leaning at almost a forty-five-degree angle to the dirt path I continued to follow. The farther I went—by now I had been climbing for three hours—the wilder the path became. Great trees had fallen down over it. Great logs interrupted its flow upward, creating huge obstacles. Great ruts carried runoff water from high up on my left to low down on my right where someplace below lay my cabin, invisible by now.

I heard strange birds screaming off in the trees that seemed to grow taller the higher I climbed. But, still I climbed, and still the path meandered up, still worn, still brown dirt, still a path, which was comforting, because if, my increasingly estranged mind thought, *if* the path would disappear, then what? Of course that would never happen. Not in a million years would that ever happen, I thought. I just left my cabin in a civilized place called Sequoia, which was only a short drive from Fresno, which was only a short drive from just about everywhere.

Which meant that, hell, I was close to Los Angeles! And I continued with that comforting thought to climb up, up, and still up.

■

It was almost four hours later that I reached the top. I could not believe it! The top! The path abruptly leveled off and I walked tentatively forward, wondering at the dramatic shift in tension in my legs and back and body. I stopped, almost terrified to look in any direction other than straight ahead of me. My body sensed that there had been something dramatic that had happened, something I was not prepared for, something I could not fully take in. Almost as a punctuation mark to that thought, a huge male deer came running down the face of the mountain on my left, across the path in front of me, and bounded off into the woods on my right. As immediately as it had appeared, it disappeared. And with it, the sound went, too.

Then I got what it was. It was the sound. There was none! The sound was completely gone. I turned to my right and for as far as the eye could see there was only space—broad open space, traveling over the huge expanse of cliffs and trees and boulders and valley stretching down, down, down as far as the eye could see.

Way off to the right rose another mountain, a long plateau of a mountain that stretched in both directions, far, far in front of me, and far, far as the eye could see behind me. And there to my left was the very same view. Space. Clear, wide, open, vaulted space stretching between the long, narrow cliffs and boulders and forests that stretched in every direction but up.

Here I was, still as a statue, standing in the place I had breezily spoken about, the word *wilderness* came to mind, and yet I had had no idea what it truly meant, until this very moment when I stopped climbing long enough to hear its awesome silence.

Here I stood, this silly, aging, childish man with not a clue as to what I had just walked into until it spoke to me and said, "So, here you are, my friend. Now what do you propose we do?"

"Do?" I thought to myself. "Do?" In one fearful second, I turned around and looked to see where I had just come from. If the first shock I had experienced just moments before was not enough, I immediately came to the realization that I had not once in the past seven hours taken a look at where I had come from. I didn't recognize the path at all! It wasn't there! There was no path, not that I could see. Not the same path that had led me to this place. Not the brown, worn path leading up, up, up.

It was gone. And with that thought, I began to run. Oh, yes, I did. Straight forward where there ran something like a path, but not the same path, no, a much different path, if it were a path at all. I started running just as the deer had done, forward, and then down, down, down, where the valley must be.

■

I arrived at my cabin at about nine that night. I was exhausted. I didn't sleep there, but quietly, and with great determination, humbled to the core, I simply picked up my stuff, put it all into the trunk of my car, and drove away from Sequoia National Park. I knew where I was going. To the ocean, near Monterey. I didn't know why, but the longer I drove, the faster I went.

The road streamed by, Sequoia grew to be farther and farther behind, and my body almost screamed with pain. I had been in the Wilderness, I knew that to be a fact. I had been in my wilderness, not the one Robinson Jeffers spoke about. Not the one Walt Whitman spoke about. But certainly the one I now knew something about. I had thrown myself out of my place of comfort to discover the one in me who was terrified of being destroyed. The one who I had kept so comfortably entertained in my life. And then, up there on the top of that space, in that cathedral of wilderness where no one else was, it was there that he woke up and said, *holy shit!* And turned us both around to start running. Without any idea whatsoever why, or where, or what. He didn't ask any questions, we didn't have a conversation about it . . . he simply woke up, said, "Holy shit!" And ran like the coward he was. "Wow, who was that guy?" I asked now as I drove like the devil to Monterey at three on a Monday morning.

■

This is what I wanted to share with you, dear reader, before this journey of ours is done. There are moments in our lives when someone wakes up in us and puts the rest of us to shame. There are moments when someone wakes up in us and does something that boggles our mind, something we cannot possibly explain. And then there are moments when we simply can't wake anyone up, no matter how hard we believe we try. The sleeping dogs lie, the sleeping dogs die. And kick them as we might, call them as we will, they are determined to sleep their lives away.

I have never gone back to Sequoia National Park since that day, but I think about it often. I think about that long stretch that stood there in front of me when I arrived at the top. I think about that huge deer running from the left to the right and disappearing right there where it seemed impossible for anything that alive and that large to disappear. I think about turning around and suddenly seeing the path that was not there, and then the urge that captured me completely to run, run, run for my life.

I see that often, and wonder what might have happened had I stayed there all night. What if I had just sat down on that path, pulled out my sleeping bag and canteen, perhaps built a little fire, and then lay down and gone to sleep? I wonder what might have happened had I chosen that path instead of the one I chose—the path that you and I are now on? I wonder, I wonder. Well, possibly something miraculous would have happened. But, strangely, I don't think anything more miraculous would have happened than the miracle that did happen. The miracle of seeing myself in a way I had never seen myself before. I saw that scared person, running for his imagined life, terrified at finding himself all alone and at risk, he thought, on the top of a strange mountain, with nothing that he knew to be true, there to comfort him. I saw him, now. I know him, now. I say to him, now, "Yes, I hear you. Yes, I do." And I will always know that you are here, you who are terrified. I will take care of you, and I will heed you, and I will engage you until that time, that very special moment, when you and I find ourselves up high, alone, and before you or I do something that time, I will say, "So, here we are again, dear friend. What do you say we get to know each other?" And he will say, "I'll try."

■

I say the same thing to you, dear reader. I say, "This is our time." I say, "There is so much to discover in this world of ours." I say, "You are not alone and there is nothing to fear. You and I can do this thing, together. You and I will see that deer in our high country, and we will say to him as he flies past, 'We're here. We're here. We're here.' "

—The End—

Or is it the beginning . . . ?

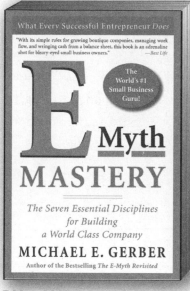